Cultural And Geographical Exploration

Building the Panama Canal

CHRONICLES FROM *NATIONAL GEOGRAPHIC*

Cultural And Geographical Exploration

Ancient Civilizations of the Aztecs and Maya
The Ancient Incas
Building the Panama Canal
Jerusalem and the Holy Land
Mysteries of the Sahara
Race for the South Pole—The Antarctic Challenge
Robert E. Peary and the Rush to the North Pole
Touring America Seventy-Five Years Ago

Cultural And Geographical Exploration

Building the Panama Canal

CHRONICLES FROM *NATIONAL GEOGRAPHIC*

Arthur M. Schlesinger, jr.
Senior Consulting Editor

Fred L. Israel
General Editor

CHELSEA HOUSE PUBLISHERS

Philadelphia

CHELSEA HOUSE PUBLISHERS

Editor in Chief Stephen Reginald
Managing Editor James D. Gallagher
Production Manager Pamela Loos
Art Director Sara Davis
Director of Photography Judy L. Hasday
Senior Production Editor Lisa Chippendale

First Printing

1 3 5 7 9 8 6 4 2

Library of Congress Cataloging-in-Publication Data

Building the Panama Canal: chronicles from National Geographic /
Arthur M. Schlesinger, Jr., senior consulting editor; Fred L. Israel,
General editor.
    cm.—(Cultural and geographical exploration)
    Includes bibliographical references and index.
    Summary: Relates the history of how the Panama Canal was planned
    and built, including political, economic, and health aspects of
    getting the project completed.
    ISBN 0-7910-5102-1 (hc.)
    Panama Canal (Panama)—History—Juvenile literature.
    [1. Panama Canal (Panama)—History.] I. Schlesinger, Arthur Meier,
    1917–   II. Israel, Fred L. III. National Geographic magazine. IV. Series.
    F1569.C2B85   1998
    972.87'5—dc21   98-44479
                                    CIP
                                    AC

CONTENTS

"THE GREATEST EDUCATIONAL JOURNAL"

When the first *National Geographic* magazine appeared in October 1888, the United States totaled 38 states. Grover Cleveland was President. The nation's population hovered around 60 million. Great Britain's Queen Victoria also ruled as the Empress of India. William II became Kaiser of Germany that year. Tsar Alexander III ruled Russia and the Turkish Empire stretched from the Balkans to the tip of Arabia. To Westerners, the Far East was still a remote and mysterious land. Throughout the world, riding the back of an animal was the principle means of transportation. Unexplored and unmarked places dotted the global map.

On January 13, 1888, thirty-three men—scientists, cartographers, inventors, scholars, and explorers—met in Washington, D. C. They had accepted an invitation from Gardiner Greene Hubbard (1822-1897), the first president of the Bell Telephone Co. and a leader in the education of the deaf, to form the National Geographic Society "to increase and diffuse geographic knowledge." One of the assembled group noted that they were the "first explorers of the Grand Canyon and the Yellowstone, those who had carried the American flag farthest north, who had measured the altitude of our famous mountains, traced the windings of our coasts and rivers, determined the distribution of flora and fauna, enlightened us in the customs of the aborigines, and marked out the path of storm and flood." Nine months later, the first issue of *National Geographic* magazine was sent out to 165 charter members. Today, more than a century later, membership has grown to an astounding 11 million in more than 170 nations. Several times that number regularly read the monthly issues of the *National Geographic* magazine.

The first years were difficult ones for the new magazine. The earliest volumes seem dreadfully scientific and quite dull. The articles in Volume I, No. 1 set the tone—W. M Davis, "Geographic Methods in Geologic Investigation," followed by W. J. McGee, "The Classification of Geographic Forms by Genesis." Issues came out erratically—three in 1889, five in 1890, four in 1891; and two in 1895. In January 1896 "an illustrated monthly" was added to the title. The November issue that year contained a photograph of a half-naked Zulu bride and bridegroom in their wedding finery staring full face into the camera. But, a reader must have wondered what to make of the accompanying text: "These people . . . possess some excellent traits, but are horribly cruel when once they have smelled blood." In hopes of expanding circulation, the Board of Managers offered newsstand copies at $.25 each and began to accept advertising. But the magazine essentially remained unchanged. Circulation only rose slightly.

In January 1898, shortly after Gardiner Greene Hubbard's death, his son-in-law Alexander Graham Bell (1847-1922) agreed to succeed him as the second president of the National Geographic Society. Bell invented the telephone in 1876 and, while pursuing his life long goal of improving the lot of the deaf, had turned his amazingly versatile mind to contemplating such varied problems as human flight, air conditioning, and popularizing geography. The society then had about 1100 members—the magazine was on the edge of bankruptcy. Bell did not want the job. He wrote in his diary though that he accepted leadership of the Society "in order to save it. Geography is a fascinating subject and it can be made interesting," he told the board of directors. Bell abandoned the unsuccessful attempt to increase circulation through newsstand sales. "Our journal," he wrote "should go to members, people who believe in our work and want to help." He understood that the lure for prospective members should be an association with a society that made it possible for the average person to share with kings and scientists the excitement of sending an expedition to a strange land or an explorer to an inaccessible region. This idea, more than any other, has been responsible for the growth of the National Geographic Society and for the popularity of the magazine. "I can well remember," recalled Bell in 1912, "how the idea was laughed at that we should ever reach a membership of ten thousand." That year it had soared to 107,000!

Bell attributed this phenomenal growth though to one man who had transformed the *National Geographic* magazine into "the greatest educational journal in the world"—Gilbert H. Grosvenor (1875-1966). Bell had hired the then 24-year-old Grosvenor in 1899 as the Society's first full-time employee "to put some life into the magazine." He personally escorted the new editor, who will become his son-in-law, to the Society's headquarters—a small rented room shared with the American Forestry Association on the fifth floor of a building, long since gone, across 15th street from the U. S. Treasury in downtown Washington. Grosvenor remembered the headquarters "littered with old magazines, newspapers, and a few record books and six enormous boxes crammed with *Geographics* returned by the newsstands." "No desk!" exclaimed Bell. "I'll send you mine." That afternoon, delivery men brought Grosvenor a large walnut rolltop and the new editor began to implement Bell's instructions—to transform the magazine from one of cold geographic fact "expressed in hieroglyphic terms which the layman could not understand into a vehicle for carrying the living, breathing, human-interest truth about this great world of ours to the people." And what did Bell consider appropriate "geographic subjects?" He replied: "The world and all that is in it is our theme."

Grosvenor shared Bell's vision of a great society and magazine which would disseminate geographic knowledge. "I thought of geography in terms of its Greek root: *geographia*—a description of the world," he later wrote. "It thus becomes the most catholic of subjects, universal in appeal, and embracing nations, people, plants, birds, fish. We would never lack interesting subjects." To attract readers, Grosvenor had to change the public attitude toward geography which he knew was regarded as "one of the dullest of all subjects, something to inflict upon schoolboys and avoid in later life." He wondered why certain books which relied heavily on geographic description remained popular—Charles Darwin's *Voyage of the Beagle*, Richard Dana, Jr.'s *Two Years Before the Mast* and even Herodotus' *History*. Why did readers for generations, and with Herodotus' travels, for twenty centuries return to these books? What did these volumes, which used so many geographic descriptions, have in common? What was the secret? According to Grosvenor, the answer was that "each was an accurate, eyewitness, firsthand account. Each contained simple straightforward writing—writing that sought to make pictures in the reader's mind."

Gilbert Grosvenor was editor of the *National Geographic* magazine for 55 years, from 1899 until 1954. Each of the 660 issues under his direction had been a highly readable geography textbook. He took Bell's vision and made it a reality. Acclaimed as "Mr. Geography," he discovered the earth anew for himself and for millions around the globe. He charted the dynamic course which the National Geographic Society and its magazine followed for more than half a century. In so doing, he forged an instrument for world education and understanding unique in this or any age. Under his direction, the *National Geographic* magazine grew from a few hundred copies—he recalled carrying them to the post office on his back—to more than five million at the time of his retirement as editor, enough for a stack 25 miles high.

This Chelsea House series celebrates Grosvenor's first twenty-five years as editor of the *National Geographic*. "The mind must see before it can believe," said Grosvenor. From the earliest days, he filled the magazine with photographs and established another Geographic principle—to portray people in their natural attire or lack of it. Within his own editorial committee, young Grosvenor encountered the prejudice that photographs had to be "scientific." Too often, this meant dullness. To Grosvenor, every picture and sentence had to be interesting to the layman. "How could you educate and inform if you lost your audience by boring your readers?" Grosvenor would ask his staff. He persisted and succeeded in making the *National Geographic* magazine reflect this fascinating world.

To the young-in-heart of every age there is magic in the name *National Geographic*. The very words conjure up enchanting images of faraway places, explorers and scientists, sparkling seas and dazzling mountain peaks, strange plants, animals, people, and customs. The small society founded in 1888 "for the increase and diffusion of geographic knowledge" grew, under the guidance of one man, to become a great force for knowledge and understanding. This achievement lies in the genius of Gilbert H. Grosvenor, the architect and master builder of the National Geographic Society and its magazine.

Fred L. Israel
The City College of the City University of New York

BUILDING THE PANAMA CANAL: AN OVERVIEW

FRED L. ISRAEL

The Panama Canal cuts through the Isthmus of Panama and links the Atlantic Ocean with the Pacific Ocean. The building of the Canal was one of the most grandiose undertakings of all time, ranking among the greatest engineering achievements in history. Its construction held the world's attention as thousands of laborers worked on it for more than ten years. They used steam shovels and dredges to cut through jungles, hills, and swamps as scientists worked to conquer such tropical diseases as malaria and yellow fever. Upon its completion in 1914, the Canal shortened a ship's voyage between New York and San Francisco to less than 5,200 miles. Previously, ships making this trip had to travel around South America—a distance of more than 13,000 miles.

The idea of a transisthmian canal was first mentioned soon after the discovery of America. As early as 1517, Vasco Núñez de Balboa, the first European to reach the Pacific, envisioned a canal connecting the Atlantic and the Pacific Oceans. During the early part of the 19th century, there were several unsuccessful efforts to form companies to build a canal. At the same time, the United States and Great Britain became involved in a number of disputes because each wanted to prevent the other from controlling possible routes. At last, in 1901, Britain gave in. The Hay-Pauncefote Treaty of that year gave the United States a free hand to build, control, and fortify an isthmian canal. The United States agreed to keep it open without discrimination to the commercial and fighting ships of all nations on equal terms.

Two routes were possible—one through Panama in the Republic of Colombia, the other through Nicaragua. In 1902, after many studies, the United States decided to use the Panama route. The Hay-Herran Treaty (1903) would have authorized the construction of the canal but the treaty was not approved by the Colombian congress. A furious President Theodore Roosevelt lost no time in declaring that the "blackmailers of Bogota" must not be allowed "permanently to bar one of the future highways of civilization."

Roosevelt encouraged Panamanian rebels to declare their independence from Colombia. With American assistance, the "revolution" succeeded. Washington promptly recognized the new Republic of Panama. The new government negotiated a treaty with the United States which allowed construction on the canal to go forward.

General George W. Goethals was chiefly responsible for supervising the construction. At the height of the work, more than 43,000 people worked on the Panama Canal. Three-fourths were blacks from the British West Indies. Other workers came from southern Europe, although most of the clerical and skilled workers were Americans. One of their greatest obstacles was disease. Colonel Williams C. Gorgas took charge of improving sanitary conditions. He began a campaign to destroy the types of mosquitoes that carried malaria and yellow fever. In fact, the first two years of canal building were devoted largely to draining swamps and clearing brush where the mosquitoes swarmed. By 1906, Gorgas had wiped out yellow fever and greatly reduced the number of deaths caused by malaria.

Within a decade of the Panamanian revolution, the Canal was completed. On August 15, 1914, the first oceangoing steamship passed through the canal. The Panama Canal gave the United States a great new enterprise to protect and broadened American involvement in the Caribbean region.

Vol. XV, No. 2   WASHINGTON   February, 1904

THE REPUBLIC OF PANAMA

By Hon. Wm. H. Burr, of the Isthmian Canal Commission

THE youngest of the American republics has almost the oldest history. The Caribbean coast line of Colombia and of Panama was one of the earliest localities visited by the old Spanish navigators. One of them, Alonzo de Ojeda, visited a number of places along this coast in 1499 and 1501, while Columbus visited Porto Bello, 25 miles northeast of Colon, and other places in 1502, during his last voyage. From those dates onward all this portion of the Spanish main was constantly visited, explored, and apportioned among Spanish officials. Many expeditions of discovery were made inland, until all that northwesterly portion of South America which has so long been known as Venezuela, Colombia, and Ecuador was completely explored and a fair knowledge of its resources, mineral and otherwise, obtained.

One of the most important incidents in these exploring expeditions occurred when Vasco Nunez de Balboa, governor of the province in Darien, first set out southward from his capital, Santa Maria de la Antigua, prompted by what the Indians had told him, and, from an elevation on the divide north of the Gulf of San Miguel, discovered the Pacific Ocean on the 25th day of September, 1513. Many of the earliest historical events of the Republic of Panama are associated with this intrepid explorer. He was on the Isthmus but a short period, but his restless energy was ever prompting him to new enterprises of exploration and aggrandizement of territory for his home government. His remarkable career was cut short in 1517 by his execution at Acla, on the Caribbean shore of the Gulf of Darien, by a jealous governor of the province, who feared that Balboa's fruitful enterprises might give him sufficient *éclat* to make him the head of the new Spanish territory in place of himself.

The Spanish discoverers found all this country, like others of South and Central America, peopled with large numbers of Indians.

The territory constituting the present Republic of Panama, as well as the northwesterly portion and west coast of South America, was carefully scoured in search of the precious metals of which fabulous stories were related by the natives, many of which were justified by subsequent results. Balboa himself visited the Pearl Islands in the Bay of Panama. These operations of the early Spaniards involved frequent crossing of the Isthmus, and even before the death of Balboa it became evident that the most practicable line of transportation was that which is now known as the Panama route.

Many attempts were made to find other practicable routes across the Isthmus between the Atrato River, emptying into the Gulf of Darien, and the Chagres River, emptying into the Caribbean Sea eight miles west of Colon; but the advantages of the Panama route were promptly recognized by the Spaniards.

A territory, consisting largely of the present Panama, Colombia, and Venezuela, was formed into the province of Tierra-firma. It was the governor of this province, Pedro Arias de Avila, who, to strengthen his authority, brought charges against Balboa, and after a form of trial executed him at Acla. By the middle of the sixteenth century large numbers of Spaniards had migrated to this country and created flourishing centers of trade. About this time, in order to secure a more suitable government for his colony, the Spanish emperor created the presidency of New Granada, which was subsequently raised to the rank of a viceroyalty in 1718, then including not only Colombia and Venezuela but Ecuador also. The territory of the Isthmus formed the northwestern arm of this Spanish appanage.

Like that of most Spanish colonies, the government of the country was corrupt, being administered largely for the benefit of the favored few in authority; but on the whole the country flourished, the population increased, and trade extended along the lines of production of the country.

THE REVOLUTION AGAINST SPANISH AUTHORITY

The course of affairs in the viceroyalty continued without much change until 1811. Many features of the Spanish rule had long borne heavily upon the people and aroused such feeling that at last they broke out into an insurrection against the home government. A continuous war against the Spanish forces sent to put down the insurrection continued until 1824, when Spanish authority disappeared. Meantime the Venezuelan patriot, Simon Bolivar, born in the city of Caracas in 1783, made his way into prominence in national affairs, and in 1819 completed a union of the three divisions of the country into the first Republic of Colombia. This republic was short lived. Venezuela withdrew in 1829 and Ecuador in 1830. The creation of the Republic of New Granada followed in 1831, but its constitution was not formed until 1832. Under it the territory was divided into eighteen provinces. The president of the new republic held office four years. The course of affairs was much disturbed, and a civil war broke out after one or two presidential terms, and did not close until 1841. In 1840 the Province of Cartagena seceded from the new republic, and immediately thereafter the neighboring provinces of Panama and Veragua took the same step. This was the first period of independence of the Isthmus of Panama. The revolting states were soon reunited under a constitution reformed in 1843. The Republic of New Granada enjoyed little tranquillity, being subject to domestic disturbances of greater or less magnitude almost continuously, but vari-

A WEDDING AT COLON

ous measures signifying general advancement in civilization were adopted from time to time. Among those was one by which slavery was entirely abolished in 1852.

An important alteration of the constitution took place in 1853, under which the provinces were merely federated into the republic, each being granted the right to assume its independence at any time. This right under the constitution was asserted by Antioquia and Panama in 1856 and 1857, this being the second independence of the Province of Panama. Stormy times followed these national upheavals, and the independence of the provinces was not long undisturbed. A congress at Bogota established a republic under the name of the United States of Colombia in 1861, adopting a new federal constitution for the purpose of including all the territory hitherto held by the Republic of Colombia, including the Isthmus of Panama. The opposite party, however, victorious in the western portion of the country, declined to acknowledge the authority at Bogota. Internal disturbances of all degrees, including the assassination of leaders and bloody battles, constituted the program until 1862, when the opposing parties came to terms to a sufficient extent to permit the appointment of a provincial government and the drawing up of a constitution. At this time another attempt, not successful, was made to reëstablish the former republic of the three countries—Venezuela, Colombia, and Ecuador; but under the constitution adopted May 8, 1863, the Republic of Colombia was erected, and it has endured to the present time. Insurrections and internal disorganizations prevailed for a number of years, and the history of the Republic has been accentuated by frequent revolutions, many of which have taken place in Panama.

EXTENT OF THE PRESENT REPUBLIC

This brings us to the consideration of the Republic of Panama as it now stands, having declared its independence on November 3, 1903. The Republic of Panama is identical in territorial limits with the department of Panama of the Republic of Colombia. This department extended from Costa Rica on the west to a line drawn first nearly due south from Cape Tiburon at the southern limit of the Gulf of Darien, then southwesterly to a point on the Pacific coast a short distance southeast of Punta Cocalito. This last or eastern limit of the department of Panama is almost entirely along the divide between the Atrato River and the watershed draining into the Gulf of San Miguel.

The Republic of Panama lies between the parallels of 7° 15′ and 9° north latitude, and also between 77° 15′ and 82° 30′ longitude west from Greenwich. Approximately speaking, therefore, its extreme length east and west is about three hundred and fifty miles, and its extreme width north and south one hundred and twenty miles. Its population is not well determined, but it probably does not extend three hundred thousand. This population is largely composed of people of Spanish descent, but there are also large numbers of negroes, who have come chiefly from Jamaica during the constructing work conducted by the old Panama Company. A few Chinamen have also found their way to the Isthmus and become permanent residents. The native Indians are also occasionally seen on the zone of population between Panama and Colon. These races have been mingled in all conceivable proportions, so that the features or racial characteristics of one or more or even all of these various nationalities may be traced in the face of a single individual. Some of the old Spanish families have still retained the purity of their blood and are among the prominent people of the Isthmus. Its entire area is about 31,600 square miles, or about the area of the State of Indiana.

The Cordillera forming the main mountain ridge extending from South to North America and constituting the continental divide runs through the entire length of the Republic of Panama, in the eastern portion the divide being much nearer the Caribbean Sea than the Pacific Ocean, while in the western portion its location is more nearly central. The low notch or saddle in the Cordillera near the city of Panama, with a summit elevation about 300 feet above sea level, the lowest throughout the Central American Isthmus except at Nicaragua, affords the railroad location built upon nearly fifty years ago and the recommended route for the isthmian ship canal.

Not less than one-half of the entire territory of the Republic is mountainous and covered with luxuriant tropical vegetation, including heavy forest trees, some of which are among the highly valuable woods. These forests are practically trackless. Tribes of Indians, not in large numbers, live along the Caribbean coast between Panama and Darien, and also on the southern slopes. Some of these Indians preserve jealously their isolation, and have never acknowledged the sovereignty of any government.

THE PANAMA RAILROAD

The most prominent feature of the Republic of Panama is the Panama Railroad and the partially constructed canal, with the adjacent strip of territory, including the cities and towns, with their aggregated business or industrial centers, along the line from Colon to Panama.

This railroad, a single-track line of five feet gauge, was built nearly fifty years ago. It is but forty-nine miles long, and it is conducted practically as an American railroad corporation, although it is owned by the new Panama Canal Company. The principal offices of the company are in the city of New York. This company does not confine itself wholly to railroad business, but owns and conducts the line of

steamers running between the ports of New York and Colon under the name of the Panama Railroad-Steamship Company.

The railroad forms a line of land transportation to which converges marine commerce from many widely separated ports of the world. On the Pacific side steamship lines plying up and down the west coast of South America, and the Pacific mail steamships touching along the North and Central America coast from San Francisco southward, together with other ships approaching from the Pacific Ocean, have made Panama their terminal port for many years. The port of Colon has an equally extensive ocean shipping business, with not less than nine or ten steamship lines from Spain, France, England, Germany, Italy, and the United States, making it either a terminal port or port of call. In addition to these ocean steamship lines there is a little coasting trade of a local character on both sides of the Isthmus carried on in small sailing vessels.

The Panama Railroad has always been a prominent transportation line, along which currents of commerce and streams of passenger traffic, fed by the steamship lines on the two oceans, have continuously flowed. Latterly a considerable banana trade has also sprung up along the railroad line.

THE RELATION OF THE ISTHMUS
TO THE REST OF THE WORLD

The location of the Isthmus is markedly central to that portion of the through commerce of the world which would be served by the Panama Canal. It is practically a half-way station between the ports of eastern Asia, Australia, and the islands between and the ports of Europe. It is believed that the opening of the canal will create a highly stimulating influence upon the trade between the west coast of South America and the ports of the United States—a business which has hitherto been developed chiefly with foreign ports. The geographical relation of the Republic of Panama to some of the principal ports of the world is shown by the following statement of the distances in nautical miles to be sailed by steam vessels on the respective trips indicated:

	Miles
From Panama to San Francisco	3,277
From Panama to Honolulu	4,665
From Panama to Yokohama	8,065
From Panama to Shanghai	8,985
From Colon to New York	1,981
From Colon to Liverpool	4,720
From Colon to New Orleans	1,380

THE RESOURCES OF THE REPUBLIC

The mineral resources of the Republic of Panama are practically undeveloped, although it is known that there are considerable deposits of coal of fair quality—perhaps of excellent quality—not far from the railroad and canal zone. The precious metals are found in small quantities at many points, with indications of greater value; but these resources, like many others of the new republic, are in such an undeveloped stage that no definite statement can be made as to their potential value.

The agricultural resources of the country are greater than ordinarily supposed. There is excellent grazing land near Colon, along the Panama Railroad, and within a few miles of the city of Panama. Further west, in the Chiriqui district, and on the Pacific side of that portion of the Isthmus, there are extensive stretches of country well adapted to agricultural purposes, both for grazing and for the raising of all those tropical products which grow in such luxuriance throughout the fertile portions of Central

America and the Isthmus. Fine grades of stock in substantial numbers are already found on some portions of the Isthmus, and dairy farming is already conducted in the vicinity of Panama.

Large stretches of native forests of valuable timber, such as mahogany, both light and dark, and other similar woods are found throughout the Republic, but are yet practically undeveloped. Such valuable tropical products as cacao, bananas of all kinds, sugar cane, indigo, cotton, tobacco, vanilla, corn, rice, and other similar products grow in abundance, and conditions of systematic industry only are needed to develop them into sources of great wealth to the country. Under the encouraging influences of a stable government, where life and property are respected, the natural resources of the Republic of Panama will be productive of an amount of wealth which, if stated in a quantitative way, would now be incredible, in view of the crude and depressed conditions of industry which have prevailed from the beginnings of its history to the present time.

COMMUNICATION

There are practically no roads found in the Republic except those of a crude and ill-kept kind near to the cities or towns along the line of the Panama Railroad Company between Colon and Panama. The only marked exception to this statement is the old so-called Royal road built between Cruces, on the upper Chagres, to Panama, a distance of about 17 miles. This old road, formerly a crude paved way, was traveled by passengers crossing the Isthmus before the construction of the Panama Railroad. This traffic found its way up the Chagres River to the small native town of Cruces, now containing a few scores of people, and then passed overland

GRINDING GRAIN

The climate of the Isthmus is thoroughly tropical in character, but it is by no means entitled to the bad name which is so frequently given to it. In speaking of this climate, all business and social activity in the Republic of Panama is so centered in the vicinity of the railroad line, which is also practically the proposed canal route, that observations as to climatic or other conditions apply strictly to this vicinity, although they are practically the same for other parts of the Republic.

At Panama the Isthmus is scarcely more than forty miles wide. The proximity of the two oceans necessarily affects the climate in a marked manner. The continental divide at this location is low, rising to an elevation but little more than three hundred feet above mean sea level. Winds therefore blow across the entire Isthmus almost unobstructed. Under the tropical sun the evaporation from the two oceans is rapid, and the consequence is an atmosphere highly charged with aqueous vapor at nearly all times. The high temperature of the tropical climate is therefore accentuated with great humidity, which is enervating to a marked degree to those who have been bred in a temperate climate.

The temperature at Colon, on the Caribbean side of the Isthmus, not often rises above 90° Fahr., although it occasionally reaches 98° or even a little higher, as in December, 1885 (98°.2), and January and March, 1886 (98°.2),

from that point either on foot or horseback, or by such crude vehicles as the country afforded, to Panama. It was by this route that many people went to California during the gold excitement of 1849 and the years immediately following. This road has been abandoned for many years, as has the ancient road from Portobello to Panama.

The greater portion of the territory of the Republic is of small elevation, with many large marshes along the seacoast. Even the mountainous portions east and southeast of the railroad, forming the Darien country, are not high, probably in no case exceeding an elevation of 2,800 feet. The arable land on either side of the Isthmus is mostly ground of low elevation.

the latter year being an unusually hot one. The mean of the maximum monthly temperature that year was 95°.2 Fahr. The usual maximum monthly temperature ranges from about 85° Fahr. to about 91° or 92° Fahr. The minimum monthly temperature usually ranges from about 60° Fahr. to about 75° Fahr., the mean minimum monthly temperature being but little under 70° Fahr. The mean temperature throughout the year is not far from 80° Fahr. The interior points of the Isthmus, such as Gamboa and Obispo, about half way across the Isthmus on the railroad line, generally experience maximum temperatures perhaps two or three degrees higher than at Colon, and minimum temperatures perhaps three or four degrees lower than at that point. On the Pacific side the temperature may run a degree or two higher than at Colon. For all ordinary purposes it may be stated that there is no sensible difference in temperature on the two sides of the Isthmus, nor in other climatic conditions except the rainfall, which differs sensibly. On the high ground at Culebra, where the canal and railroad lines cut the continental divide, and where the elevation is from two hundred to three hundred feet above sea level, the air is cooler and dryer than at either seacoast. These figures show that the ruling temperatures on the Isthmus are not so high as those shown by the hottest weather of a New York or Washington summer; but the temperatures, such as they are on the Isthmus, continue without material abatement.

The low latitude of the Isthmus of Panama, the farthest point north lying in latitude 9°, brings the sun at the zenith twice during the year, once at noon on April 13 on its journey northward, and the second time at noon on August 29 on its return southward toward the winter solstice. At the summer solstice its eleva-

tion above the north horizon is 75° 41′ and 57° 24′ above the south horizon at the winter solstice. These conditions introduce an approach to uniformity in the temperature of the varying seasons, as they also produce opposite prevailing winds in different portions of the year. As the direct rays of the sun tend to cause the hot air to rise vertically under it during those portions of the year when the sun is north of the zenith, the prevailing winds are southerly or southwesterly, but when it is south of the zenith the same causes make the prevailing winds from north or northeasterly. It is in this portion of the year when at rare intervals the northers blow into the harbor of Colon with such severity as to require ships found in it to put to sea for their safety.

The year on the Isthmus is divided into the dry season and the wet season. The dry season covers the four months of January, February, March, and April, during which little or no rain falls. The wet season is composed of the remaining eight months of the year, the wettest portions being usually in May and in October. The rainfall on the Caribbean side—*i. e.*, at Colon—is considerably greater than either in the interior or on the Pacific side, its annual amount usually ranging from about 85 to nearly 155 inches, with an average of about 125 to 130 inches. In the interior, as at Gamboa or Bas Obispo, the annual precipitation varies ordinarily from about 75 to nearly 140 inches, with an average of 90 to 95 inches. The total precipitation at Panama, however, may vary from about 45 to about 85 inches per annum, with an average of about 66 to 67 inches. As the average annual precipitation in New York or Washington may vary approximately from 40 to 50 inches, it is seen that the wet season in the Republic of Panama exhibits relatively high rainfall, although not more than about one-half of that which occurs at Greytown, in Nicaragua.

During the wet months there are some phenomenal downpours, with the effect of turning rivers into torrents, and this is particularly the case with the Chagres River, the principal river of the Republic, which empties into the Caribbean Sea about 8 miles west of Colon. Passing up this river from its mouth, its general course lies southeast for a distance of nearly 30 miles to Obispo. Still passing up stream, its course at this point turns sharply to the northeast. From Obispo for a distance of about 23 miles down stream the course of the Panama Railroad and the line of the proposed canal follow the Chagres River to the low lands adjoining the Caribbean coast. In the other direction, however, both the railroad and the canal leave the river at Obispo and cut through the continental divide toward Panama, the Panama end of the canal being about 20 miles from Obispo.

THE VARIOUS PROJECTS
FOR A SHIP CANAL

At the present time the greatest interest centering on the Republic of Panama, aside from the remarkable unanimity with which the people of the Isthmus as a unit declared and secured their independence through a single, effective but bloodless effort, is that which attaches to the proposed ship canal connecting the two oceans practically along the line of the Panama Railroad. The project of an Isthmian ship canal is almost as old as the discovery of the Isthmus, for it is nearly 400 years ago that the Spaniards themselves seriously discussed this enterprise. As early as 1520 the Spanish monarch, Charles V, directed a survey to be made for the purpose of determining the feasibility of an isthmian ship canal. From that time until this the project of a ship canal across the Isthmus has been actively discussed, although as a result of that early survey the Spanish governor declared "that such a work was impracticable, and that no king, however powerful he might be, was capable of forming a junction of the two seas or of furnishing the means of carrying out such an undertaking." The followers of the Spanish governor were less easily discouraged than he.

The ship-canal enterprise gathered advocates from one century to another, until, during the nineteenth century and the first years of the twentieth, many careful surveys of possible routes across the Isthmus were made. The principal of those lying in the Republic of Panama, beginning with the most easterly, are the Caledonia route, the San Blas route, and the Panama route. The Caledonia route has at times attracted much attention on account of the highly colored but absolutely false accounts rendered of it by one or two early explorers. The northern extremity of this route, at Caledonia Bay, is about one hundred and sixty-five miles east of Colon and crosses the Isthmus in the main in a southwesterly direction. The surveys of the Isthmian Canal Commission showed that the elevation of the divide at this point and the heavy work to be done along its line were far too great to permit its feasibility being considered in comparison with that of the Panama route. The San Blas route, the Caribbean end of which is on the Gulf of San Blas, is about sixty miles east of Colon. This route has the distinguishing characteristic of being located on probably the shortest line between the tide waters of the two oceans on the Isthmus, this distance being scarcely thirty miles. The short length of this line has secured for it a

LOW TIDE IN THE HARBOR OF PANAMA;
THE RANGE OF TIDE AT PANAMA IS 20 FEET, AND AT COLON ONLY ONE FOOT

number of earnest advocates. It also was subject to survey by the engineering parties of the Isthmian Commission. The elevation of the divide at this crossing is so great as to necessitate the consideration of a ship tunnel from five to seven miles long, the canal being planned as a sea-level waterway. The great cost of a canal on this line and the hazards attending such a construction as a ship tunnel rendered this route, like the Caledonia line, neither practicable nor feasible, compared with the Panama route.

Many surveys and examinations have been made at different crossings of the Central American isthmus between Tehuantepec, in Mexico, and the eastern limit of the Republic of Panama. As earnest and as enthusiastic as the supporters of other routes have been, the most complete and exact surveys and estimates have shown that the Panama route embodies the

ONE OF THE HOSPITAL BUILDINGS ON THE HILL BACK OF PANAMA

greatest number of advantages of any line ever considered for a ship canal between the two oceans. It is a tribute to the sagacity and good judgment of the old Spanish explorers that they also settled upon practically this route as the most feasible and practicable for the same purpose.

The proposed Panama line, favorably reported upon by the Isthmian Canal Commission and now adopted as the basis of the treaty being negotiated between the United States and the Republic of Panama, begins at Colon and extends in a southeasterly direction to a point on the Bay of Panama near the city of that name, and has a total length of 49.07 miles between the six-fathom curves in the two oceans. At the present time the city of Colon has a population of probably about 3,000 people, while the city of Panama has a population of perhaps 25,000 people. The population scattered along the line of the railroad may add ten to fifteen thousand more, making a total of perhaps forty to forty-five thousand people in the 10-mile strip of territory between the two oceans within which the railroad is found and the canal will be built.

THE PLAN OF DE LESSEPS

This canal route is that which was adopted at the International Scientific Congress convened in Paris in May, 1879, under the auspices of Ferdinand de Lesseps, the concession for the canal having been obtained from the Republic of Colombia in the preceding year by Lieut. L. N. B. Wyse, a French naval officer. This congress not only selected the Panama route, but also decided that the waterway to be constructed should be a sea-level canal. A company entitled "Compagnie Universelle du Canal Interocéanique," and commonly known as the Old Panama Canal Company, was immediately organized to construct the work. After various efforts it financed the enterprise and began work, which was prosecuted until May 15, 1889, when the company went into bankruptcy, and its effects were put into the hands of a liquidator, an officer of the French court corresponding closely to the American receiver.

Prior to the bankruptcy of the old company the project for a sea-level canal was temporarily abandoned in the hope that the funds available might be sufficient for the construction of a lock canal. After various vicissitudes the new Panama Canal Company was organized on the 20th of October, 1894. Work was resumed on the canal immediately thereafter, and has been continued until the present time, the force employed, however, being small. The old company raised by the sale of stocks and bonds not far from $246,000,000, and it has been stated that the number of persons holding the securities was over two hundred thousand.

When the concession for building the Panama Railroad was secured from the Colom-

bian Government, control of all available transportation routes across the Isthmus in the territory of the present Republic of Panama was covered by it. The construction of the ship canal by the old Panama Canal Company was therefore subject to the rights conveyed in the Panama Railroad concession. In order to control this feature of the situation, therefore the old Panama Company purchased nearly the entire stock of the railroad company, which thus became a part of the assets of the new Panama Canal Company.

THE RECOMMENDATIONS OF THE ISTHMIAN COMMISSION

When the Isthmian Canal Commission made its first visit of investigation of the canal routes four years ago, it found a large amount of excavation and other work done along the line of the canal, as well as a large amount of land, buildings, structures, and many plans and papers, all constituting a part of the property of the new Panama Canal Company. All this property was situated on the Isthmus except a mass of plans and papers in the office of the canal company at Paris. The Commission in its report, under date of November 16, 1901, recommended, in case of selection of the Panama route, payment of $40,000,000 to the new Panama Canal Company for all its property, rights, and concessions connected with the unfinished canal. That offer, as made by the United States Government, has since been accepted by the French company.

The Isthmian Canal Commission adopted the French line for its estimates, but made some material changes in the plans for the work. The canal as planned by the Commission is a lock canal, its typical or standard section for firm earth having a bottom width of 150 feet, a

A MARKET SCENE IN PANAMA

minimum depth of water of 35 feet, and a top width of 269 feet. This section is suitably modified for harbor sections, for sections in soft ground, for sections in rock and in lakes and wherever required by unusual conditions. These adopted sections would afford ample waterway for the greatest ships afloat at the present time, as required by the law creating the Commission.

The locks for this canal are great masonry constructions, having a usable length of 740 feet with a clear width of 84 feet, more than large enough to accommodate any vessel now afloat or planned to be built.

Beginning at the 6-fathom curve in the harbor of Colon, the canal is planned to be excavated for a distance of 7 miles through the low, marshy grounds in that vicinity to Gatun, where the line meets the Chagres River. From that point to Bohio, about 17 miles from Colon, a little east of south from the point of starting, the canal would be excavated generally along the marshy lowlands through which the Chagres River flows in that vicinity, cutting the course of that river four or five times. This 17-mile section of the canal is a sea-level section, but at Bohio is found a comparatively narrow place in the valley of the Chagres River with rock outcroppings on one side and at which a dam may be built. At this point it was the purpose of the French company also to build a dam, but the Isthmian Canal Commission provisionally located its dam at a site nearly half a mile downstream from that of the French dam, and proposes to build it materially higher.

THE GREAT DAM AT BOHIO

This dam would retain behind it the waters of the Chagres River at an elevation varying from 85 feet to 90 or 92 feet above mean sea level, thus forming what has been called Lake Bohio. It would back up the water of the Chagres River for a distance of about 20 miles, through about 14 of which the course of the canal would be laid. Lake Bohio would constitute the summit level of the canal, and would be reached by two great masonry locks built together, *i. e.*, in series near one end of the dam at Bohio, the lift of each one of these two locks being 45 feet as a maximum. These locks would be built as twin structures, so that if an accident should happen to one side the other side would still be available for use, and thus save the operation of the canal from being broken. A great ledge of rock affords an excellent site for the construction of these locks.

The building of this great dam at Bohio, with its top nearly 100 feet above the water in the river in its normal condition, is one of the great works of the entire canal construction. As the safety and operation of the canal would depend entirely upon the stability of this dam, the commission recommended a plan of construction by which a masonry core wall 30 feet thick at the bottom and 8 feet at the top would be built up from the rock beneath the bed of the river to the top of the dam, thus efficiently preventing all leakage of water through the porous sand and gravel, of which large portions of the substrata beneath the river bed are composed.

As the top of this dam would have an elevation of 100 feet above the sea, and as the highest water in Lake Bohio would be 8 feet lower than that elevation, no water would ever overflow this dam, but the surplus of flood waters of the Chagres River would be discharged over a masonry spillway about 3 miles from the dam. The spillway weir would be of masonry and about 2,000 feet long. Its location is in a notch or depression in the ridge between the headwaters of a small tributary of the Chagres called the Gigante and the valley of the Chagres River. The crest of this 2,000-foot-long overflow would be 85 feet above sea level. It is estimated that with the greatest flood possible in the Chagres River the depth of water on the overflow weir would not be greater than 7 feet. During a great flood, therefore, the river would discharge into this lake, and its waters would accumulate there until deep enough to run over the masonry spillway. With the flood in a rising stage, the amount flowing over the spillway would increase up to the greatest flood height, after which the rate of discharge over the spillway would decrease. This regulation of the Chagres floods, therefore, takes care of itself. It requires no attention. After discharging over the spillway, the flood waters would flow through an artificial channel down into the Chagres River beyond any of the canal works and where no damage would be done.

About 10 miles up the Chagres from Obispo at a point called Alhajuela there is an excellent site for a dam. It has been proposed to build at this Alhajuela site a great masonry dam for the purpose of impounding flood waters of the Chagres River to the extent of the storage capacity behind the dam, and so reduce the flood effects in Lake Bohio. This storage reservoir would also act as a source of feed water for the canal should the traffic on it in the future become so large as to require this additional supply.

THE CULEBRA CUT

From Obispo, 30 miles from Colon, the canal line runs toward the southeast through the continental divide in a direct course toward Panama, and for nearly 7 miles from Obispo a great cut has to be made through the high ground forming that divide. For a distance of about 5 miles from Obispo this is known as the Emperador Cut, beyond which lies a mile and a half known as the Culebra Cut. The greatest depth of this cut at Culebra is about 250 feet, and the amount of material to be removed in this stretch of 7 miles of canal excavation is about 43,000,000 cubic yards. It is the greatest single feature of the entire canal construction.

CUTTING THE CANAL THROUGH MORASSES, CHAGRES RIVER REGION

THE CULEBRA CUT

The summit or Bohio Lake level ends at a point called Pedro Miguel, about 1½ miles southeasterly of the Culebra Cut and 38 miles from Colon, where is located a flight of two locks arranged in twin plan like the others, each one of the pair having a lift varying from 27 to 31 feet, according to the varying height of water in Lake Bohio. By means of these two locks the water surface in the canal is brought down to an elevation about 28 feet above sea level. The last lock on the line is at a point called Miraflores, a little less than a mile and a half from the Pedro Miguel locks. From Miraflores to the end of the canal, at a point called La Boca on the Bay of Panama, is less than 5 miles, and this portion of the canal constitutes what may be called the Pacific section or level. The water of this Pacific section of the canal rises and falls coincidently with the tides in the Bay of Panama, and as the range of tide in that bay is about 20 feet, the Miraflores lock is largely a tidal lock. Its minimum lift, therefore, at high tide, is 18 feet, while the maximum lift at low tide is 38 feet. It is obvious from these tidal conditions that if the canal were constructed as a sea-level canal a tidal lock would be needed at or near its Pacific end. That part of the canal line between Miraflores and the Bay of Panama is located closely along the course of the Rio Grande, which is mainly a tidal river, its two principal tributaries above Miraflores being Rio Pedro Miguel and Rio Caimitillo, both being small and insignificant streams.

The length of canal between the shore lines is about 44 miles, although the length between the 6-fathom curves on the two sides of the Isthmus, as has already been stated, is 49 miles, 13 of which lie in the artificial Lake Bohio. The creation of Lake Bohio would necessitate the relocation and rebuilding of the railroad between Bohio and Obispo, throwing it back upon higher ground.

No canal with locks can be operated without provision for the water used in taking boats through the locks, for evaporation, for seepage, and for other purposes incident to maintenance and operation of the canal. At each lockage on the Panama canal a lock full of water, representing a volume nearly 750 feet long, 84 feet wide, and 45 feet deep, would be used in the Bohio locks and about two-thirds as much in the Pedro Miguel locks. This requires a large supply of water, which the Isthmian Commission computed for all purposes to be 1,070 cubic feet per second for an annual traffic of 10,000,000 tons passing through the canal. This water supply is afforded by the Chagres River, and without it or its equivalent the canal would not be possible.

In view of the complete system of self-control of the Chagres floods by the Gigante Spillway, the Chagres River, instead of being an insurmountable obstacle to the construction and maintenance of the canal, as has at times been apprehended, is actually a gracious feature of the canal environment, and by that automatic control it has been changed from a sinister agent to a friendly power. Furthermore, while the average discharge of the Chagres River is nearly three times the quantity required for feeding the canal, there are times in the dry seasons when the discharge of the river is not more than two-thirds of the quantity required for that purpose. This deficiency is abundantly made up by the storage in Lake Bohio until the traffic exceeds 10,000,000 tons annually. At that time the storage in the Alhajuela reservoir will give an additional supply for an increase of traffic three or four times as great as the volume which can be accommodated by the storage in Lake Bohio.

ABOMINABLE SANITARY CONDITIONS

The sanitary conditions of the Isthmus are at the present time wretchedly bad. Neither Colon nor Panama has either a system of water supply or a sewer system. The water used in Panama for potable purposes is brought into the city in casks mounted on wheels and drawn by mules from some more or less polluted source outside of but near the city, or caught in cisterns from the rain water flowing from roofs during the wet season, or in some other crude and usually unsanitary way.

There are a few drains in the city of Panama, constructed immediately under the surface of the streets, with little or no regard to grades. The water or sewage and decaying matter collecting in the low portions of these drains and remaining there under the high temperature of the climate make them far worse than no drains at all. The lack of care and proper disposal of household and other refuse creates the most unsanitary conditions imaginable. These observations may be emphasized for the smaller towns and villages between Colon and Panama. As a consequence, yellow fever is probably always present, and at times assumes epidemic form. Malarial fevers and other similar diseases are also continually present under aggravated forms. These conditions, however, are completely remediable by means well known and available at the present time.

The entire Isthmus can be placed in a completely sanitary condition so that its healthfulness shall be assured by resorting to methods and means which have now become practically standard in the sanitation of cities and towns. It is absolutely essential that water works, supplying potable and wholesome water, be established for the cities and larger towns, and concurrently therewith there must be established suitable sewer systems with rational and sanitary disposal of sewage. All these results are now perfectly practicable of attainment without unreasonable cost or material difficulty. It will be imperative, however, that sanitary regulations be created, enforced, and maintained with the rigor of military discipline. Under such reasonable sanitary conditions as it is entirely practicable to attain, and with proper quarantine regulations, there is no reason why the Isthmus may not be maintained entirely free of yellow fever or from other tropical epidemics.

COST OF THE CANAL

The United States Government has entered into a provisional agreement to purchase the entire property of every description and the rights of the new Panama Canal Company for the sum of $40,000,000. The cost of completing the Panama Canal under the plan of the Isthmian Canal Commission is estimated by that Commission at $144,233,358. The sum of these two amounts—$184,233,358—represents the total cost of the construction of the isthmian ship canal by this route, to which should be added such additional costs as are required to be incurred in securing the additional rights and concessions necessary to enable the United States Government to enter upon the Isthmus and begin the work.

The consummation of this great work is apparently close at hand. The creation of the Republic of Panama has solved the difficulties which had gathered about the negotiations of the requisite treaty, and it will probably be but a short time before this, the greatest engineering work of the world, will be undertaken and carried to completion. This achievement will not only create new lines of ocean commerce and stimulate some of the older lines into new life, but it will also bring the Atlantic and Pacific shores of the United States into much closer communication than before, thus strengthening those bonds of mutual interest and natural sympathy which lie at the foundation of best national life. In this part of the world's development the new Republic of Panama becomes the center of the material activities through which these great results will be accomplished, thus attaining the fruition of 400 years of effort. She is to be congratulated in marking her entrance among the nations of the earth by opening the way to the attainment of this world improvement and giving the work the impetus of her national sanction.

THE PANAMA CANAL

By Lieut. Col. Geo. W. Goethals, U. S. Army

Chairman and Chief Engineer, Isthmian Canal Commission

The following article was submitted to President Taft by Colonel Goethals, March 16, as a special report on the Panama Canal situation. The report gives such a complete and clear review of why the lock type of canal is being constructed that we publish it in full.

A CANAL connecting the Atlantic and Pacific Oceans has occupied public attention for upward of four centuries, during which period various routes have been proposed, each having certain special or peculiar advantages. It was not until the nineteenth century, however, that any definite action was taken looking toward its accomplishment.

In 1876 an organization was perfected in France for making surveys and collecting data on which to base the construction of a canal across the Isthmus of Panama, and in 1878 a concession for prosecuting the work was secured from the Colombian Government.

In May, 1879, an international congress was convened, under the auspices of Ferdinand de Lesseps, to consider the question of the best location and plan of the canal. This congress, af-

ter a two weeks' session, decided in favor of the Panama route and of a sea-level canal without locks. De Lesseps's success with the Suez Canal made him a strong advocate of the sea-level type, and his opinion had considerable influence in the final decision.

Immediately following this action the Panama Canal Company was organized under the general laws of France, with Ferdinand de Lesseps as its president. The concession granted in 1878 by Colombia was purchased by the company, and the stock was successfully floated in December, 1880. The two years following were devoted largely to surveys, examinations, and preliminary work. In the first plan adopted the canal was to be 29.5 feet deep, with a ruling bottom width of 72 feet. Leaving Colon, the canal passed through low ground to the valley

SKETCH MAP SHOWING PANAMA CANAL AND
GATUN LAKE

of the Chagres River at Gatun, a distance of
about 6 miles; thence through this valley, for 21
miles, to Obispo, where, leaving the river, it
crossed the continental divide at Culebra by
means of a tunnel, and reached the Pacific
through the valley of the Rio Grande. The difference in the tides of the two oceans, 9 inches
in either direction from the mean in the Atlantic and from 9 to 11 feet from the same datum
in the Pacific, was to be overcome and the final
currents reduced by a proper sloping of the bottom of the Pacific portion of the canal. No provisions were made for the control of the
Chagres River.

In the early eighties after a study of the flow
due to the tidal differences a tidal lock near the
Pacific was provided. Various schemes were also
proposed for the control of the Chagres, the
most prominent being the construction of a dam
at Gamboa. The dam as proposed afterward
proved to be impracticable, and this problem remained, for the time being, unsolved. The tunnel through the divide was also abandoned in
favor of an open cut.

THE FIRST CHANGE FROM THE SEA-LEVEL TO THE LOCK TYPE

Work was prosecuted on the sea-level canal until 1887, when a change to the lock type
was made, in order to secure the use of the canal for navigation as soon as possible. It was
agreed at that time that the change in plan did
not contemplate abandonment of the sea-level
canal, which was ultimately to be secured, but
merely its postponement for the time being. In
this new plan the summit level was placed above

the flood line of the Chagres River, to be supplied with water from that stream by pumps. Work was pushed forward until 1889, when the company went into bankruptcy; and on February 4 that year a liquidator was appointed to take charge of its affairs. Work was suspended on May 15, 1889. The New Panama Canal Company was organized in October, 1894, when work was again resumed, on the plan recommended by a commission of engineers.

This plan contemplated a sea-level canal from Limon Bay to Bohio, where a dam across the valley created a lake extending to Bas Obispo, the difference in level being overcome by two locks; the summit level extended from Bas Obispo to Paraiso, reached by two more locks, and was supplied with water by a feeder from an artificial reservoir created by a dam at Alhajuela, in the upper Chagres Valley. Four locks were located on the Pacific side, the two middle ones at Pedro Miguel combined in a flight.

A second or alternative plan was proposed at the same time, by which the summit level was to be a lake formed by the Bohio dam, fed directly by the Chagres. Work was continued on this plan until the rights and property of the new company were purchased by the United States.

THE UNITED STATES BECOME INTERESTED

The United States, not unmindful of the advantages of an isthmian canal, had from time to time made investigations and surveys of the various routes. With a view to government ownership and control Congress directed an investigation of the Nicaraguan Canal, for which a concession had been granted to a private company. The resulting report brought about such a discussion of the advantages of the Panama route to the Nicaraguan route that by an act of Congress, approved March 3, 1889, a commission was appointed to—

"make full and complete investigation of the Isthmus of Panama, with a view to the construction of a canal . . . to connect the Atlantic and Pacific Oceans . . . and particularly to investigate the two routes known respectively as the Nicaragua route and the Panama route, with a view to determining the most practicable and feasible route for such canal, together with the approximate and probable cost of constructing a canal at each of the two or more of said routes."

The commission reported on November 16, 1901, in favor of Panama, and recommended the lock type of canal. The plan consisted of a sea-level section from Colon to Bohio, where a dam across the Chagres Valley created a summit level 82 to 90 feet above the sea, reached by two locks. The lake or summit level extended from Bohio to Pedro Miguel, where two locks connected it with a pool 28 feet above mean tide, extending to Miraflores, the location of the final lock. The ruling bottom width of the canal prism was fixed at 150 feet, increased at the curves and in the submerged channels. In Panama Bay the width was fixed at 200 feet, and in the artificial channel in Limon Bay 500 feet was adopted, with turning places 800 feet wide. The minimum depth was 35 feet, and the locks were to have usable lengths of 740 feet and widths of 84 feet. The commission assessed the value of the rights, franchises, concessions, lands, unfinished work, plans, and other property, including the railroad of the New Panama Canal Company, at $40,000,000.

By act of Congress, approved June 28, 1902, the President of the United States was authorized to acquire, at a cost not exceeding $40,000,000, the property rights of the New Panama Canal Company on the Isthmus of

Panama, and also to secure from the Republic of Colombia perpetual control of a strip of land not less than 6 miles wide, extending from the Caribbean Sea to the Pacific Ocean, and—

"the right . . . to excavate, construct, and to perpetually maintain, operate, and protect thereon a canal of such depth and capacity as will afford convenient passage of ships of the greatest tonnage and draft now in use."

In event the provisions for the purchase and for securing the necessary concession from Colombia could not be carried out, the President was authorized to secure the rights necessary for the construction of the Nicaraguan Canal.

The law also provided, after the foregoing arrangements had been perfected, that–

"the President shall then, through the Isthmian Canal Commission . . . cause to be excavated, constructed, and completed a canal from the Caribbean Sea to the Pacific Ocean. Such canal shall be of sufficient capacity and depth as shall afford convenient passage for vessels of the largest tonnage and greatest draft now in use, and such as may be reasonably anticipated."

To enable the President to carry out these provisions certain sums were appropriated and a bond issue, not to exceed one hundred and thirty millions of dollars, was authorized. By this act Congress, in accepting the estimates accompanying the report of the commission of 1901, adopted the type proposed by the board, or a lock canal.

Pursuant to the legislation, negotiations were entered into with Colombia and with the New Panama Canal Company, with the end that a treaty was made with the Republic of Panama granting to the United States control of a 10-mile strip, constituting the Canal Zone, with the right to construct, maintain, and operate a canal. This treaty was ratified by the Re-

public of Panama on December 2, 1903, and by the United States on February 23, 1904.

The formal transfer of the property of the New Panama Canal Company on the Isthmus was made on May 4, 1904, after which the United States began the organization of a force for the construction of the lock type of canal, in the meantime continuing the excavation by utilizing the French material and equipment and such labor as was procurable on the Isthmus.

THE INTERNATIONAL BOARD OF EXPERTS

The question of a sea-level canal was again agitated, and secured such recognition that the President convened an international board of engineers, consisting of 13 members, to assemble at Washington on the 1st day of September, 1905, for the purpose of considering the various plans for the construction of the canal that would be submitted to it.

The plans submitted may be briefly summarized as—

(1) That of the commission of 1901, which has already been explained.

(2) A lock canal with terminal lakes proposed by Mr. Lindon W. Bates, and for which three projects were proposed. The one which he appeared to favor contemplated a summit level of 62 feet above the sea, created by a dam at Bohio, and an intermediate level of 33½ feet above mean tide. effected by a dam at Mindi. This plan provided four locks—at Mindi, Bohio, Pedro Miguel, and Sosa. A variant of the plan contemplated a dam at Gatun instead of at Bohio, showing that, at least for a 30-foot head, the Gatun location was not considered by him as unfavorable or offering any difficulties respecting the foundations. His other plans were modifications of this, the summit levels being

27 or 62 feet, but in each instance the lock type was advocated.

(3) The plan proposed by Mr. Bunau-Varilla carried out the ideas of the first French company, namely, the construction of a lock canal with a summit level 130 feet above mean tide, to be ultimately converted into a sea-level canal, or what he calls the Straits of Panama. The locks were to be constructed so that as the levels were deepened by dredging they could be eliminated, navigation continuing during the enlargement and transformation. The material removed by the dredges was to be deposited in the lake formed of the upper Chagres River by a dam at Gamboa, and any suitable locations in the various pools between the locks. In commenting on this plan the Board of Consulting Engineers concluded that—

"After a full and careful consideration of all the features of Mr. Bunau-Varilla's plan, the board is of the opinion that it should not be adopted for the Panama Canal for the following reasons::

"1. The construction of the large locks required under the present law and necessary for the accommodation of the traffic seeking the canal after its completion makes it quite impossible to complete the preliminary lock canal even nearly within the period stated.

"2. The excessive cost of transformation added to the loss of costly locks and other appurtenant structures required by the preliminary lock canal.

"3. If the lock canal is likely to be retained for many years, it should be made for the most efficient service, and not be encumbered with modifications in lock construction which would prove inconvenient in use."

(4) A plan proposed by Maj. Cassius E. Gillette, a lock canal with a summit level 100 feet above mean tide by the construction of a dam across the Chagres Valley at Gatun.

No sea-level plan was submitted for consideration, so that the board outlined a general plan of its own, and for purposes of comparison adopted as the lock type a 60-foot summit level canal. Two levels were used; the summit level was carried by an earth dam at Bohio, and the intermediate level by an earth dam at Gatun, each dam sustaining a head of 30 feet. It is to be noted that no difficulties were anticipated in the construction of these dams, and there was no dread or fear of the foundations.

As the result of its deliberations, the board submitted a majority report and a minority report signed by five of its members, the former advocating a sea-level canal and the latter a lock canal, with the summit level 85 feet above mean tide.

THE LOCK TYPE IS ADOPTED

The Isthmian Canal Commission, with one dissenting voice, recommended to the President the adoption of the lock type recommended by the minority, which was also strongly advocated by the then chief engineer, Mr. John F. Stevens. The President, in the message to Congress dated February 19, 1906, stated:

"The law now on our statute books seems to contemplate a lock canal. In my judgment a lock canal, as herein recommended, is advisable. If the Congress directs that a sea-level canal be constructed its direction will, of course, be carried out; otherwise the canal will be built on substantially the plan for a lock canal outlined in the accompanying papers, such changes being made, of course, as may be found actually necessary, including possibly the change recommended by the Secretary of War as to the site of the dam on the Pacific side."

On June 29, 1906, Congress provided that a lock type of canal be constructed across the Isthmus of Panama, of the general type proposed by the minority of the Board of Consulting Engineers, and work has continued along these lines. As originally proposed, the plan consisted of a practically straight channel 500 feet wide, 41 feet deep from deep water in the Caribbean to Gatun, where an ascent to the 85-foot level was made by three locks in flight. The level is maintained by a dam approximately 7,700 feet long, one-half mile wide at the base, 100 feet wide at the top, constructed to 135 feet above mean tide. The lake formed by this dam, 171 square miles in extent, carried navigation to Pedro Miguel, where a lock of 30 feet lift carried the vessel down to a lake 55 feet above mean tide, extending to Sosa Hill, where two locks overcame the difference of level between the lake surface and the Pacific. Nineteen and eight-hundredths miles of the distance from Gatun to Sosa Hill had a channel 1,000 feet at the bottom, a minimum channel for 4½ miles through Culebra of 200 feet at the bottom. The balance of the distance varied in width to 800 feet, the larger portion of the entire canal being not less than 500 feet. The depth of water was fixed at 45 feet. The lake assured a perfect control of the Chagres River.

IMPROVEMENTS
IN THE ORIGINAL PLANS

Certain changes have been made in the original project, the most important being the withdrawal of the locks from Sosa to Miraflores, which was recommended and adopted in December, 1907. This resulted in a change in the direction of the channel in Panama Bay. A breakwater is being constructed from Sosa to Naos Island which, by cutting off the silt-bearing cross-current, which has always been troublesome, protects the channel against silting.

A second change is the widening of the 4½ miles of Culebra cut to a width of 300 feet at the bottom. This was done by Executive order and was not made on the recommendation of the commission.

A third change is the location of the breakwaters in Colon Harbor. The necessity for these breakwaters was made apparent in the latter part of January, when a storm of some magnitude seriously interfered with shipping. As originally proposed for both the sea-level and lock types, the breakwaters were parallel to the axis of the channel excavated in Limon Bay. If so constructed, sufficient area would not be given to dissipate the waves entering head on into the channel, and they would not afford much, if any, protection to shipping. These breakwaters are to be built out from Manzanillo Island and Toro Point, so as to give a sheltered anchorage, and also an opportunity for such expansion to the waves as to break them up.

A fourth change is in the dimensions of the locks. As proposed by the minority they were 900 feet by 95 feet, usable lengths and widths. These dimensions were subsequently changed by the commission at the instigation of the President to dimensions 100 feet wide and 1,000 feet long. The width was again increased to 110 feet on the recommendation of the General Board of the Navy, so as to accommodate any possible increase in beam of future battleships.

SENSATIONAL AND MISLEADING STORIES ABOUT THE GATUN DAM

The Gatun dam is to consist of two piles of rock 1,200 feet apart and carried up to 60 feet above mean tide. The space between them and up to the required height is to be filled by selected material deposited in place by the hydrau-

GREAT BLAST IN PROGRESS
25 holes; 19.5 tons dynamite; material displaced, 70,769 cubic yards

lic process. During the construction of the north side of the south rock pile a slip occurred in November last at the crossing of the French Canal. This was the fifth slip that occurred at this point, the rock settling to some extent, but generally slipping sidewise until the angle of re-

pose was reached. In this connection it is to be noted that the silt deposits in the channel had not been removed. This slip would probably have passed unnoticed, as did the former ones, but for the fact that at the time a flood in the Chagres River had attained such proportions as to cover a portion of the Panama Railroad tracks just south of Gatun. A newspaper correspondent, going from Colon to Panama, saw his opportunity for a sensational story, and attributed the flood to the dropping of the Gatun dam into the subterranean lake under the dam and locks, which another faker had previously discovered, and the news of the destruction of the Gatun dam was cabled to the States.

The slip did not affect the south slope or side of the rock pile. It was entirely local and did not in any way interfere with the work. It would not have occurred had steps been taken during construction to give the proper slope to the rock pile, but economy of time and money did not warrant such precaution. As stated by one of the engineering publications, "We can state from actual personal examination that this incident has absolutely no engineering significance."

As a result, however, the public is told that dire disaster will follow the undertaking unless the present plans are abandoned and the Straits of Panama constructed—that is, a sea-level canal across the Isthmus 500 to 600 feet wide. To accomplish this, however, a lock canal must be built first, and subsequently widened and deepened until the ideal is reached. There is no data available for such a canal. With mountains instead of hills to be removed estimates are, of course, impossible; so the most optimistic figures, suitable alone to the ideal, are offered as a bait. In any event it is also claimed that Bohio should have been selected for the site of the dam in lieu of Gatun.

As between Gatun and Bohio, at both places the distance from the natural surface to the rock is so great that any attempt to found the dam on the last-named material will be attended by enormous expense. At Bohio the

gorge in its lower strata is filled with water-bearing gravel, and to make the dam safe the underflow through these strata would have to be cut off by some means extending down 165 feet. No such strata exist at Gatun, so, for this reason alone, leaving out of consideration the advantages in the control of the Chagres River and to navigation by reason of the greater extent of lake, Gatun offers the better site.

Both the majority and minority of the Board of Consulting Engineers considered Gatun a suitable location for a dam; the former adopted it for the typical lock canal used for comparison with the sea-level canal, the latter for the 85-foot summit-level canal. The majority, however, feared the existence of an underground flow in case of the higher dam, but investigations have failed to disclose any. The great mass of underlying material is not sandy and gravelly deposits, as was supposed, but a mixture of these materials so firmly cemented together with clay as to make the strata in which they occur impervious to water.

THE FOUNDATION OF THE DAM AND LOCKS AT GATUN IS SATISFACTORY

I venture the statement, without fear of contradiction, that the site of no public or private work of any kind has received such a thorough and exhaustive examination and investigation as the foundation of the dam and locks at Gatun. There is no longer a doubt concerning any of the underlying strata; neither the impermeability nor the ability of the foundations to bear the loads that will be brought upon them can be questioned if the data be carefully and impartially examined. The investigations fail to disclose any water-bearing strata or the existence of that underground stream with a discharge equal to the Chagres River itself, which was recently asserted as a fact on the floor of the Senate.

In this connection the statement is also made that the change in the location of the locks at the Pacific end was due to our demonstrated inability to construct the dams, and that as the foundation at Gatun is of the same material, it necessarily followed that the Gatun dam is also impossible of accomplishment.

The majority of the Board of Consulting Engineers in its report states that—

"The dam at La Boca, between San Juan Point and the Sosa Hill, unless carried down to bed rock at that location, would be placed upon a far worse founda-

LOW TIDE NEAR THE PACIFIC TERMINUS OF THE CANAL

EXCAVATING FOR THE SITE OF THE GREAT GATUN DAM, LOOKING SOUTH

There are now on the Isthmus forty-eight 95-ton, forty-two 70-ton, ten 45-ton, and one 38-ton steam shovels, or a total of one hundred and one steam shovels.

tion than that proposed at Gatun or Mindi. The La Boca site is one covered by an ooze of mud or silt, with some sandy material overlying the rock. . . . Unless some feature equivalent to that of a heavy masonry core characterized the design of the dam at this point, or unless a resort be made to dredging down to bed rock or near to it, and refilling with suitable material, or an earth dam at this location be made very massive, it would be in grave danger of being pushed bodily out of place by the pressure due to the head of water in the reservoir."

We found the material in the foundations of these dams not only worse than at Gatun, but in nowise comparable. In the former a covering of ooze and silt, in the latter firm ground with a few soft or marshy spots.

THE LOCKS ORIGINALLY PLANNED FOR LA BOCA WERE WITHDRAWN FOR MILITARY REASONS

I know that the La Boca dams could be built to safely withstand the heads of water in the resulting lake by adopting either the method of dredging out the ooze or by giving massive dimensions to the superimposed structure. The engineering committee and the majority of the commission preferred the former method. In either case the cost would exceed the original estimates, and in addition it is a military blunder to push the locks to and beyond the proper line of defense, especially when the canal is a military necessity to this country. That the dams could be built is evidenced by the fact that the west toe of the Sosa-Corozal dam was carried across the valley on the ooze as an embankment for a railroad to be utilized in transporting stone for the Pacific locks. The charge, therefore, that the dams could not be constructed is not true, and the analogy at Gatun does not follow. Nor is there any truth in the statement that the military necessity was an afterthought, as has been insinuated.

I visited the Isthmus in 1905 with a committee of the Board of National Coast Defenses, with which I was associated at that time, for a study of the defenses of the canal. When the location of the locks at the Pacific end was fixed I was directed to call the Secretary of War's attention to the military necessity of withdrawing the locks to the interior. This I did, with the result that in forwarding the report of the Board of Consulting Engineers to the President he calls attention to the fact as follows:

> "The great objection to the locks at Sosa Hill is the possibility of their destruction by the fire from an enemy's ship. If, as has been suggested to me by officers of this department entitled to speak with authority on military subjects, these locks may be located against and behind Sosa Hill in such a way as to use the hill as a protection against such fire, then economy would lead to the retention of this lake. . . . If, however, Sosa Hill will not afford a site with such protection, then it seems to me wiser to place the locks at Miraflores."

In forwarding the report to Congress, the President calls attention to the change recommended by the Secretary of War in the location of the locks on the Pacific side. The so-called afterthought appears, therefore, as a

conclusion reached long before I had any connection with the work.

WHY THE GATUN DAM WAS REDUCED IN HEIGHT

Discredit is also thrown on the Gatun dam because there has been a desire to reduce the height from 135 to 105 feet. The original height was arbitrarily fixed to secure an excess of weight, so as to fully compress the underlying material, supposed to be largely silt deposited by the river. Subsequent investigations show that the supposed compressibility does not exist; that a marine, not a river deposit is encountered. The greater the height of the dam the greater the difficulty of constructing the upper portion, and the greater the cost, both in time and money. From present available data, if the lake should take the total discharge of the Chagres River, the water surface would not exceed 90 feet; the top of the locks, 92 feet above sea-level, would permit escape of the water long before it could reach the crest of the dam. Why then go to the expense of the extra height of the dam, and what is to be gained thereby? Assuming the crest of the dam as 100 feet wide, uniform slopes from the rock piles would give a height of 105 feet, and this height was suggested. Because as an additional reason it was mentioned that the pressure over the base would be more uniformly distributed by a dam with the cross-section proposed, the opponents of the present project, without ascertaining the facts, point to the change as a desire to secure a uniform base pressure, and use it as an argument against the stability of the foundation.

Much also has been made of the fact that in the testimony before one of the congressional committees mention was made of secur-

CLOSING OF THE CHAGRES RIVER AT GATUN

A single steam shovel at work on the Panama Canal recently removed 3,941 cubic yards of rock and earth in a working day of eight hours. This breaks all records for a single day's excavation by one steam shovel. The shovel was actually at work 6 hours and 50 minutes.

ing the stability of the superstructure by balancing the dam on the underlying material. Naturally the testimony is read and discussed in such a way as to leave the impression that the entire dam is to be so constructed. The ground to be covered by the dam is crossed by three water-courses, the Chagres River, the French Canal, and the West Diversion, and between these streams the ground is undulating, Spillway Hill reaching a height of 110 feet above sea-level. It is not remarkable or unprecedented that there should be depressions which undrained become soft with the excessive rainfall. Except for these, the ground is firm. It is in the crossing of these soft spots that slips have occurred

and are liable to occur, and to which the balancing method referred. They are relatively small in extent and when drained or filled cause no trouble, as experience at the La Boca embankment clearly proves.

As previously stated, the Gatun dam satisfactorily solves the problem of the control of the Chagres, and there should be no doubt in the mind of any one who impartially examines the data that the solution is not only feasible, but absolutely safe. As there has never been any question raised as to the safety and stability of the dams at Pedro Miguel and Miraflores, with the Gatun dam accepted, other things being equal, the relative merits of the lock *versus* sea-level canal must rest upon the ease and safety of navigation offered by the two types.

THE SEA-LEVEL TYPE MAKES NO PROVISION FOR CONTROLLING THE FLOODS OF THE CHAGRES RIVER

In the sea-level type offered in lieu of the lock type already described, the Chagres River is controlled by a masonry dam across the valley at Gamboa 4,500 feet long, 750 feet of which is subject to a pressure due to a head of 170 feet during the extreme flood stages of the river. Proper sluice gates are proposed for discharging the river into the canal. The difference in tides is overcome by means of a lock on the Pacific side in the vicinity of Sosa Hill. While provisions are made for damming or diverting some of the streams that would otherwise enter the canal prism, not less than 22 flow directly into the canal, with no provision to control the currents or check the deposits of material carried by them during flood stages.

The prism of the canal is to have a bottom width of 150 feet through the earth sections, or for nearly one-half its length, and a 200-foot bottom width through the rock sections. Nineteen miles of the length are made of curves, so that the proposed sea-level canal is not a wide, straight, and open channel, connecting the two oceans, but a narrow, tortuous ditch, with varying currents of unknown strength, impeded by a lock, and threatened by a dam resisting a pressure due to a head twice as great as that at Gatun.

To be sure, the partisans of the sea-level type are now proposing to eliminate both the Gamboa dam and the tidal lock by making the channel so wide as to reduce the currents that result from the discharge of the Chagres and the difference in tides, but fail to explain how they purpose to control or divert the Chagres, the bed of which will be 50 feet above the water surface of the canal at the juncture. As data is not available for preparing accurate estimates for even such a sea-level type as was originally offered, neither they nor any one else can offer any figures as to time and cost for the construction of such a canal as they now advocate.

In any comparison, therefore, we must confine our attention to the lock type as now building and a sea-level canal as offered by the board of engineers and not by the idealist.

FOR OUR BATTLESHIPS AND SHIPS OF COMMERCE THE LOCK TYPE IS QUICKER AND SAFER

So far as the two prisms are concerned, for ease and safety of navigation the lock type is better because of the greater widths of channels, fewer and easier curves, and freedom from objectionable and troublesome currents, both from the Chagres and its tributaries. This must be admitted by all, but the exponents of the sea-level type concentrate their attention on the obstructions and dangers that the locks constitute in the lock type, and also on the dangers that will result from the failure of the Gatun dam, forgetting that at least equally great disaster must follow the failure of the Gamboa dam. The lock in the sea-level canal is not mentioned, probably because the danger is not so great, since there is but one.

Experience shows that the risks to ships in narrow waterways are material and important. In such a channel as the original Suez Canal the delays and losses to commerce were great, and the danger to ships considerable; although the benefit of the widening is striking, this is true even now.

It is well known that the narrow channels connecting the Great Lakes have been obstructed repeatedly by vessels aground or wrecked in such a manner as to block traffic. Even in the entrances to our seaports there is a frequency of accidents which illustrate the difficulties encountered in navigating narrow and tortuous channels.

Accidents in locks have been relatively few, and none of a serious nature have occurred at the Saint Marys Falls Canal during fifty-four years of its use. The risks to ships in such a narrow waterway as proposed for the sea-level canal at Panama far outweigh all hazards in the proposed lock canal, provided the latter is built so as to minimize the chance of accident at the locks. This is met by providing every possible safety device, by building the locks in duplicate, and by the installation of a system by which the vessels will be controlled by powerful electric machinery on the lock walls, thus avoiding mistakes on the part of the vessel's crew or engine-room staff, which once led to an accident at the Manchester Ship Canal.

Again, it is objected that the size of the locks limits the canal to vessels which can use them. This is true. The present lock designs provide intermediate gates dividing the locks into lengths of 600 and 400 feet. About 98 per cent of all the ships, including the largest battleships now building, can be passed through the 600-foot lengths, and the total lock length will accommodate the largest commercial vessels now building, which I believe are 1,000 feet long and 88-foot beam.

It is true that ships may increase in size so as to make the present locks obsolete, but the largest ships now afloat can not navigate the present Suez Canal nor the proposed sea-level canal at Panama. It must also be remembered that the commerce of the world is carried by the medium-sized vessels, the length of only one of the many ships using the Suez Canal being greater than 600 feet.

The General Board of the Navy is on record that 110-foot width will be ample for the future needs of the Navy, and naval construction of the future will be limited not alone by the locks of the Panama Canal, but also by the available dry docks. Ships that can not use locks 1,000 feet by 110 feet can not use a 150-foot sea-level canal, nor can this be so easily and economically increased and maintained as is made to appear by its advocates.

Increasing the width of Culebra cut, as recently ordered, from 200 to 300 feet is advanced as an argument to show that the locks are too narrow. Ships do not navigate the locks in the sense that they do the canal prism, and the wider the channel the easier will be navigation. On account of slides that developed in Culebra cut considerably more additional work was made necessary in the upper reaches of the divide than was contemplated, and the advantages of the increased width to navigation were so great, compared with the relative amount of material to be removed in order to secure it, that the President ordered it. By this action the width of the locks is in nowise called into question.

THE GATUN LAKE WILL NOT LEAK THROUGH THE HILLS

The water supply for lockages was so exhaustively treated by the minority of the board that it has not been called into question by any one who has carefully considered the report and data submitted therewith. Recently, however, the theory has been advanced that the water of the lake may seep through the adjacent hills or through the bottom, and is significantly referred to as a mooted question. This possibility is emphasized by the seamy quality of the rock when exposed. The French plans, with Bohio Lake, were the result of careful and protracted study and investigation, and nothing of the kind was anticipated. The commission of 1901 was not in doubt of the resisting power of the hill covering such a flow. The report of the geologist on the general formation of the country does not lead to any such dread or fear. The reservoirs, constructed in the hills of the same geological formation as the entire lake area, are not affected by any such leakage or seepage. At Black Swamp, an extensive area between Bohio and Gatun, the water stands above the level of the Chagres—which is within half a mile—and also above sea-level the level of the water remains unchanged, clearly indicating no such leakage.

Toward the close of the last dry season certain measurements of the Chagres at Bohio indicated a less discharge there than at Gamboa; this was subsequently exploded by other observations which showed that the first ones were in error. Notwithstanding this, and in spite of the many evidences of the tightness of the earth covering, the possibility of a flow through the hills was advanced and was seized upon as another argument against the lock type.

A SEA-LEVEL CANAL WOULD PROBABLY COST TWICE AS MUCH AS THE LOCK CANAL

The Board of Consulting Engineers estimated the cost of the lock type of canal at $139,705,200 and of the sea-level canal at $247,021,000, excluding the cost of sanitation, civil government, the purchase price, and interest on the investment. These sums were for construction purposes only.

I ventured a guess that the construction of the lock type of canal would approach $300,000,000, and without stopping to consider that the same causes which led to an increase in cost over the original estimates for the lock canal must affect equally the sea-level type, the advocates of the latter argued that the excess of the new estimates was an additional reason why the lock type should be abandoned in favor of the sea-level canal.

The estimated cost by the present commission for completing the adopted project, excluding the items let out by the Board of Consulting Engineers, is placed at $297,766,000. If to this be added the estimated cost of sanitation and civil government until the completion of the work, and the $50,000,000 purchase price, the total cost to the United States of the lock type of canal will amount to $375,201,000. In the preparation of these estimates there are no unknown factors.

The estimated cost of the sea-level canal for construction alone sums up to $477,601,000, and if to this be added the cost of sanitation and civil government up to the time of the completion of the canal, which will be at least six years later than the lock canal, and the purchase price, the total cost to the United States will aggregate $563,000,000. In this case, however, parts of the estimate are more or less conjectural—such as the cost of diverting the Chagres to permit the building of the Gamboa dam and the cost of constructing the dam itself. Much has been said of the disadvantage of the seamy rock in connection with some experiments made at Spillway Hill test pit and of the so-called "indurated clay," yet these same disadvantages ap-

A STREET IN PANAMA BEFORE THE AMERICAN RENOVATION
This street formed one of the plague spots.

ply to the foundation at Gamboa, and the same class of material must be dealt with. The cost of constructing and maintaining a channel through the swamps of the lower Chagres is an unknown factor, and no schemes have been developed for controlling the various streams that are encountered and that must be reckoned with along the route of the canal. So that the sea-level estimates have not the accuracy of those for the lock type.

The majority of the Board of Consulting Engineers estimated that from ten to thirteen years would be required for the completion of the sea-level canal. The Isthmian Canal Commission and the then Chief Engineer fixed the time from eighteen to twenty years. It will take at least six years to complete the dam at Gamboa, and until the control of the Chagres River is assured, little if any excavation can be carried lower than 40 to 50 feet above sea-level; so that, in the absence of anything more definite, the time needed to construct the Gamboa dam is assumed as the additional period needed for completing the sea-level type.

THE SAME STREET AFTER IT HAD BEEN RECONSTRUCTED
BY THE AMERICAN GOVERNMENT
All the streets of Panama and Colon have been renovated in the same manner.

THE COST OF THE CANAL EXCEEDS THE ORIGINAL ESTIMATES BECAUSE OF UNFORESEEN CONTINGENCIES

Much criticism has resulted because of the excess of the present estimates over those originally proposed, arising largely from a failure to analyze the two estimates or to appreciate fully the actual conditions.

The estimates prepared and accompanying the report of the consulting engineers were based on data less complete than are available at present. The unit costs in the report of 1906 are identical with those in the report of 1901, and since 1906 there has been an increase in the wage scale and in the cost of material. On the Isthmus wages exceed those in the United States from 40 to 80 percent for the same class of labor. The original estimates were based on a ten-hour day, but Congress imposed the eight-hour day. Subsequent surveys and the various changes already noted have increased the quantity of work by 50 per cent, whereas the unit costs have increased only 20 per cent—not such a bad showing. In addition, municipal improvements in Panama and Colon, advances to the Panama Railroad, and moneys received and deposited to the credit of miscellaneous receipts aggregate $15,000,000, which amount will eventually and has in part already been returned to the Treasury. Finally, no such system of housing and caring for employees was ever contemplated as has been introduced and installed, materially increasing the overhead charges and administration.

DREDGING DEVICES IMPRACTICABLE

Much stress has been laid upon the fact that recent improvements in machinery have so modified conditions that the excavation can be done more economically by special devices in conjunction with dredging than is possible with the methods now adopted. The machines referred to are for shattering rock under water, and, though it is claimed that such devices have given satisfactory results in connection with the Manchester Ship Canal, it is known that similar appliances have failed in certain localities in the United States where they were tried. The variations in the character of the rock on the Isthmus from soft argillaceous sandstone to hard trap are such as to make the use of such devices very problematical. Experience generally has shown that more money can be wasted on subaqueous rock excavation than in the removal of such material in the dry. Experiments are now being made on the Isthmus with one of these rock-crushing devices, but thus far the results are not promising.

PROBABLE EFFECT OF EARTHQUAKES

Much has been written recently concerning the probable effect of earthquakes. The last earthquake of any importance occurred in the seventeenth century, and existing ruins in

Panama demonstrate clearly that no shock of any violence could have occurred during the eighteenth or nineteenth centuries. Should an earthquake visit the Isthmus the chances are that the effect upon the Gatun dam would be less disastrous than upon the Gamboa dam. The solid concrete construction of the locks, strengthened by reënforcements, will be as proof against any earth shocks as any structure which man builds anywhere, and the sea-level canal has as much to fear as the lock canal.

The vulnerability of the lock canal in time of war is another argument advanced in favor of the sea-level type, but has little weight, as the sea-level type is equally vulnerable from attacks by land or air in its Gamboa dam as are tidal locks and the various devices for controlling the streams along the route.

THE OPEN DITCH, FROM SEA TO SEA, AN IMPOSSIBILITY

The idea of the sea-level canal appeals to the popular mind, which pictures an open ditch offering free and unobstructed navigation from sea to sea, but no such substitute is offered for the present lock canal. As between the sea-level and the lock canal, the latter can be constructed in less time, at less cost, will give easier and safer navigation, and in addition secure such a control of the Chagres River as to make a friend and aid of what remains an enemy and menace in the sea-level type.

In this connection attention is invited to the statement made by Mr. Taft, when Secretary of War, in his letter transmitting the reports of the Board of Consulting Engineers:

"We may well concede that if we could have a sea-level canal with a prism of 300 to 400 feet wide, with the curves that must now exist reduced, it would be preferable to the plan of the minority, but the time and cost of constructing such a canal are in effect prohibitive."

We are justly proud of the organization for the prosecution of the work. The force originally organized by Mr. John F. Stevens for the attack upon the continental divide has been modified and enlarged as the necessities of the situation required, until at the present time it approaches the perfection of a huge machine, and all are working together to a common end. The manner in which the work is being done and the spirit of enthusiasm that is manifested by all forcibly strikes every one who visits the works.

The main object of our being there is the construction of the canal; everything else is subordinate to it, and the work of every department is directed to the accomplishment of that object.

In addition to the department of construction and engineering, there are the departments of sanitation and civil administration, the quartermaster's and subsistence departments, the purchasing department organized in the United States, the legal department, and the departments of examination of accounts and disbursements. Subordinated to, but acting in conjunction with, the commission is the Panama Railroad.

THE CANAL ZONE HAS BECOME ONE OF THE HEALTHIEST REGIONS IN THE WORLD

Too much credit cannot be given to the department of sanitation, which, in conjunction with the division of municipal engineering, has wrought such a change in the conditions as they existed in 1904 as to make the construction of the canal possible. This department is subdivided into the health department, which has charge of the hospitals, supervision of health matters in Panama and Colon, and of the quarantine, and into the sanitary inspection department, which looks after the destruction of the mosquito by various methods, by grass and brush cutting, the draining of various swampy areas, and the oiling of unavoidable pools and stagnant streams.

According to the statistics of the health department, based on the death rate, the Canal Zone is one of the healthiest communities in the world, but in this connection it must be remembered that our population consists of men and women in the prime of life, with few, if any, of the aged, and that a number of the sick are returned to the United States before death overtakes them.

To the sanitary department are also assigned 11 chaplains employed by the commission to attend the sick, as well as to look after the spiritual welfare of the employees. At most of the villages there is a combined church and lodge house, so constructed that the lower floor is used for divine service, while the upper part provides places for meetings of the various lodges. The assignment of time to ministers and to lodges is made by the quartermaster's department.

The department of civil administration exercises supervision over the courts, which consist of three circuit and five district judges; the three former, sitting *in banc*, constitute the supreme court. The district courts take cognizance of all cases where the fine does not exceed $100 or imprisonment does not exceed thirty days. Jury trials are restricted to crimes involving the death penalty or life imprisonment—in short, summary justice rules, and so long as the zone is nothing more nor less than a construction camp this form of law or justice will continue to be the most satisfactory.

The department of civil administration has charge also of the police force, the post-offices, collection of customs and taxes, the issue of licenses, and the public school system. The schools are improved to such an extent that the children of the employees have very nearly the same advantage as in the United States up to and including the high-school courses.

THE LABORERS

The quartermaster's department has charge of the recruiting of labor, the care, repair, and maintenance of quarters, the collection and disposal of garbage and refuse, the issue of furniture, and the delivery of distilled water and commissary supplies to the houses of employees, and is to have charge of the construction of all new buildings. Operating in conjunction with the purchasing department in the States, the quartermaster's department secures all supplies needed for construction and other purposes and makes purchases of materials on the Isthmus when required.

The common-labor force of the commission and the Panama Railroad aggregates in the neighborhood of 25,000 men, and consists of about 6,000 Spaniards, with a few Italians, the remainder being from the West Indies. The Spaniard is the best laborer, as he possesses more strength and endurance. Under some conditions this is not true, the foreigner strenuously objecting to doing work that requires him to stand in water.

All the skilled labor, the clerical force, and the higher officials are Americans and are recruited through the Washington office.

This department also has charge of all the property records, receives semi-annual returns of property from all those to whom property has been issued, and checks the returns and inventories of the storehouses, made at certain times, with the records compiled from original invoices.

THE HOTELS AND MESSES FOR THE MEN

The subsistence department has charge of the commissaries and the manufacturing plants, which consist of an ice and cold-storage establishment, a bread, pie, and cake bakery, a coffee-roasting outfit, and a laundry. These belong to the Panama Railroad Company, as, at the time they were established, money received from sales could be reapplied, whereas if operated by the commission the money would have reverted to the Treasury, necessitating reappropriation before the proceeds of sale could be utilized. They are, however, under the management of the subsistence officer of the commission, who has charge of the various hotels, kitchens, and messes of the commission.

There are 16 hotels from Cristobal to Panama, which serve meals to the American, or gold, employees at 30 cents per meal. There are 24 messes where meals to European laborers are served, the cost per day to such laborers being 40 cents; and there are 24 kitchens, or messes, for meals supplied to the silver laborers, or West Indians, the cost to the laborer being 30 cents per day for three meals. Subsistence is furnished without profit to the commission, though every effort is made to have the institutions self-supporting. The commissaries and manufacturing plants are operated at a profit, so as to reimburse the Panama Railroad Company for its outlay in six years from January 1, 1909, at 4 per cent interest.

The subsistence department also has charge of the Hotel Tivoli, which is a large hotel lo-

A BASQUE FROM SPAIN, WORKING ON THE CANAL

In the month of March, 1909, there were actually at work 31,071 men, 24,911 for the Commission, and 6,160 for the Panama Railroad Company. Of the 24,911 men working for the Commission, 4,278 were on the gold roll, which comprises those paid in United States currency, and 20,633 men on the silver roll, which comprises those paid on the basis of Panaman currency on its equivalent. Those on the gold roll include mechanics, skilled artisans of all classes, clerks, and higher officials, most of whom are Americans; those on the silver roll include principally the common laborers, who are practically all foreigners. Of the 6,160 Panama Railroad employees, 838 were on the gold roll.

cated at Ancon, for the entertainment of the commission s employees at a comparatively low rate, and of transient guests at rates usually charged at first-class hotels.

All moneys are handled by the disbursing officer, who pays accounts that have been previously passed upon by the examiner of accounts. This last-named official makes the administrative examination required by law prior to the final audit of the accounts by the Auditor for the War Department. The pay rolls are prepared from time books kept by foremen, timekeepers, or field clerks, subsequently checked by the examiner of accounts, who maintains a force of time inspectors. The time inspectors visit each gang, generally daily, at unknown times to the foreman, timekeeper, or field clerk, and check the time books with the gangs of workmen; the inspectors report to the examiner of accounts the results of their inspection not only in connection with timekeeping, but all violations of the regulations of the commission that may come under their observation.

Payments of payrolls are made in cash, beginning on the 12th of each month and consuming four days for the entire force on the Isthmus. All American employees and European laborers are paid in gold; all on the so-called "silver roll" are paid in Panamanian silver.

THE ENGINEERING DEPARTMENT

The department of construction and engineering is under the direct charge of the Chief Engineer. He is assisted by the Assistant Chief Engineer, who considers and reports upon all engineering questions submitted for final action. The Assistant Chief Engineer has charge of the designs of the locks, dams, and spillways, and supervision of these particular parts of the work. There is attached to the Chief Engineer an assistant to the Chief Engineer, who looks after mechanical forces on the Isthmus and has supervision over the machine shops, the cost-keeping branch of the work, the apportionment of appropriations, and the preparation of the estimates. There is also an assistant engineer, who has charge of all general surveys, meteorological observations, and river hydraulics.

The zone is divided territorially into three divisions, each in charge of a division engineer, the first extending from deep water in the Caribbean south to include the Gatun locks and dams, known as the "Atlantic Division." The second, or "Central Division," extends from Gatun to Pedro Miguel, and includes the excavation through the continental divide. The third, or "Pacific Division," extends from Pedro Miguel, including the locks and dams of that locality, to deep water in the Pacific.

The general plans emanate from the office of the Chief Engineer and the details are left to division engineers, subject to the approval of the Chief Engineer. The whole idea of the organization in the department of construction and engineering, and in fact of all the work, is to place and fix responsibility, leaving to each subordinate the carrying out of the particular part of the work intrusted to his charge.

Each division engineer has charge not only of the work involved in the construction of the canal, but all municipal engineering, including water supply, building and maintaining roads, and the establishment and maintenance of sewer systems. With the force under his charge the division engineer executes such sanitary draining as may be prescribed by the chief sanitary officer, so that all construction work, excepting the construction of buildings, concerning the location of which the division engineer is con-

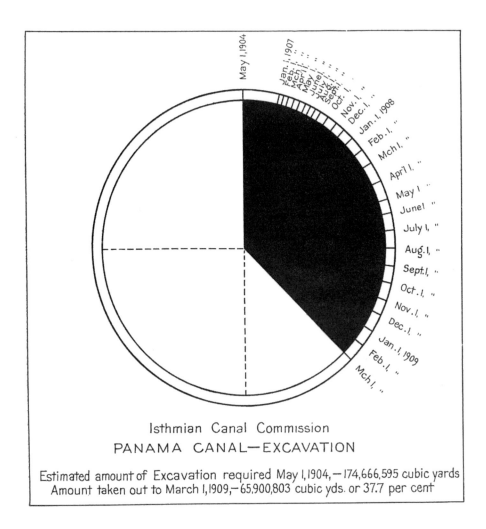

Isthmian Canal Commission
PANAMA CANAL—EXCAVATION

Estimated amount of Excavation required May 1,1904,—174,666,595 cubic yards
Amount taken out to March 1,1909,—65,900,803 cubic yds. or 37.7 per cent

sulted, however, is directly in the hands of the division engineer.

THE Y. M. C. A.

Attached to the office of the chairman is a general Y. M. C. A. secretary, who has supervision of the commission's club-houses, which are operated and maintained under the auspices of the Y. M. C. A. Four of these are now con-structed and in operation, and four more are to be built from funds recently made available by Congress. They have done much toward securing a greater permanency to the force, in giving healthful amusement, and to a better contentment on the part of the employees.

I have endeavored to show that a channel of sufficient width, in which the waters of the many streams, especially the Chagres, will not be a menace, is one most desired for an Isthmian Canal. The sea-level canal proposed by the majority of the Board of Consulting Engineers is not of sufficient width, nor is the proposed solution for the impounding and diversion of the Chagres and other streams based upon sufficient investigations to insure its success. The "ideal" sea-level canal, the Straits of Panama, recently proposed, is not based upon any investigations of the work to be done and cannot, in view of the approximate estimate of the cost of our own sea-level canal, which is about one-third the size of the "ideal" plan, be given serious consideration. Every criticism against the stability of our locks or dams can be attributed to either an argument in favor of one's own plans or to absolute ignorance of the exhaustive data concerning their safety now in existence. The several other plans of lock-type canal have nothing in their favor that the plan now adopted does not possess to a greater degree.

I have endeavored also to show that the organization on the Isthmus is compact and complete in every way, performing its duties of construction, sanitation, and government with clock-like precision. I cannot do better than quote from the message recently sent to the Congress, "that hereafter attack on this type—the lock type—is in reality merely attack upon the policy of building any canal at all," for the adoption of a sea-level canal anywhere approaching the ease of navigation of the lock type will result in the ultimate abandonment of the canal; and I assure you that several years hence, no later than January 1, 1915, even the most ardent sea-level advocates will, in making the voyage through the canal, admit that the ability to navigate a battleship at a high rate of speed through the lake and wide channel from Gatun to Pedro Miguel far outweighs the small inconveniences of the safe lockages up to and down from the summit level.

THE PANAMA CANAL*

BY COLONEL GEORGE W. GOETHALS, CHIEF ENGINEER OF THE PANAMA CANAL

It is not possible in the time at our disposal to enter upon a description of the explorations and investigations which were made of various routes proposed for a canal joining the two oceans, nor can an account be taken of the considerations which resulted in the United States finally adopting the Panama route. Suffice it to say that under the Spooner Act, approved June 28, 1902, the President of the United States secured the necessary concession from the Republic of Panama, purchased the rights and property of the New French Canal Company, and undertook the construction of the canal on May 4, 1904.

The Isthmus of Panama runs nearly east and west, and the canal traverses it from Colon on the north to Panama on the south, in a general direction from northwest to southeast, the Pacific terminus being 22 miles east of the Atlantic entrance.

*An address to the National Geographic Society, February 10, 1911.

TORRENTIAL FLOODS OF THE CHAGRES RIVER

The greatest difficulty of the Panama route is the control or disposition of the Chagres River and its tributaries. The Chagres River rises in the San Blas Mountains and drains a basin of 1,320 square miles, about half of which is above the mouth of the Obispo River. Its course is generally parallel to the Caribbean coast line so far as the mouth of the Obispo, where it turns almost at right angles to the westward, pursuing this general course to Tabernilla, whence it traverses a tortuous channel in a general northwesterly direction and enters the Caribbean Sea to the west of Limon Bay.

The general elevation of the valley is but little above sea-level to Bohio, where the low-water surface of the Chagres is one foot above mean tide. At the mouth of the Obispo, 13 miles from Bohio, the low-water surface is 48 feet above, and at Alhajuela, 11 miles farther, it is 95 feet above the same datum. Above Bohio the Chagres Valley is undulating, the hills becoming higher and steeper as the river is ascended,

A STREET IN THE CITY OF PANAMA
AS IT APPEARED WHEN THE UNITED STATES OBTAINED CONTROL OF THE CANAL

causing very rapid run-off of the rains, amounting to 100 inches and over in eight or nine months, the average duration of the wet season.

The maximum observed rainfall is 5.86 inches in one hour; the greatest recorded change in the river at Gamboa is a rise of 25.6 feet in 24 hours. Its discharge at the beginning of the rise was 8,200 cubic feet per second, increasing to 90,000 cubic feet per second at the peak of the flood. The excessive rainfall and precipitous character of the hills enclosing the valley make it a torrential stream. The bars formed during floods differ materially, and are of sand, gravel, pebbles, and rounded stones three inches to six inches in diameter. The sand and clay deposits are useful in giving suitable material for the impervious portion of the dams, while the gravel beds furnish ballast for the railroad and for other purposes.

The Chagres River has 26 tributaries between Bas Obispo and Gatun, the largest of which are the Gatun and Trinidad rivers, the former entering from the east with a drainage basin of about 160 square miles, and the latter from the west, draining an area of about 390 square miles. Each rises in the same character of country as the Chagres, and though with

THE SAME STREET REPAIRED BY THE AMERICAN ADMINISTRATION

All the streets of Panama and Colon have been renovated in a similar manner. Many miles of macadamized roads have also been built in outlying districts.

smaller drainage areas, they are of the same torrential character and must be reckoned with in the general question of the control of the Chagres and its tributaries.

Various methods for the disposition or control of the Chagres have received consideration. The first French company, in its attempt to cut a sea-level canal, found it necessary to provide diversion channels to care for the water of the rivers. The New Panama Canal Company adopted the plan of a dam across the river valley at Bohio, creating a lake above this point and discharging the flood waters to the level below

by means of a spillway in the adjacent hills. The canal which the President was authorized to construct by the provisions of the Spooner Act was the lock type recommended by the first Isthmian Canal Commission in its report submitted November 16, 1901. This plan also provided a lake for controlling the Chagres by a dam at Bohio, following along the plans of the New Panama Canal Company, thereby utilizing to the fullest extent the work already accomplished.

Early in the progress of the work the construction of a sea-level canal was agitated; this is undoubtedly the ideal canal. It took such a hold on the public mind that, in consideration of the international importance of the work, the President convened a Board of Consulting Engineers to consider and report upon the type of canal which should be adopted. This Board consisted of 13 members—five representatives of European countries and eight Americans—and assembled in Washington in June, 1905. The minority of this Board—five in number—reported in favor of the lock type for the reasons that such a canal would provide greater safety for ships and less danger of interruption to traffic by reason of its wider, straighter, and deeper channels, as well as quicker passage for large ships; the other considerations were that such a canal could be built in less time and for less money.

In forwarding the report of this Board to Congress, on February 19, 1906, the President stated: "The law now on our statute books seems to contemplate a lock canal. In my judgment a lock canal as herein recommended is advisable." On June 29, 1906, the Congress authorized the construction of the lock type of canal, in accordance with the general plans of the minority of the Board, and the work has since been carried on along these lines.

This conclusion was not generally accepted as satisfactory; the plan was again vigorously attacked after the settlement and slip in a part of one of the toes of the Gatun Dam in the latter part of 1908, and the "Battle of the Levels" continued well into 1909, notwithstanding the fact that the then President-elect, with a party of eminent engineers, after a personal inspection of the work advocated no change.

WISDOM OF CHOICE OF LOCK CANAL NOW GENERALLY ACKNOWLEDGED

Since then, as the work has advanced, the wisdom of the choice is clearly shown and there is no doubt as to the ultimate success of the project. Developments within the last year in the form of slides have brought more prominently to the front the excellence of the judgment which accepted the minority plan in lieu of the sea-level plan as advocated by the majority, and show more clearly the greater difficulties that would be encountered in an attempt to construct a sea-level canal.

An English scientist, who has kept in close touch with the work since the Americans took charge, and who at first was skeptical as to the Gatun Dam, said, after a recent visit, that he was converted to the present plan because it is not a dam at all that is building, but a veritable hill. He also thought that the expressed opinion of the Board of Consulting Engineers with reference to the Gatun Dam, namely, "that no such vast and doubtful experiment should be indulged in," was now applicable to Culebra Cut. There are probably some who still believe a wrong choice was made, but a visit to the Isthmus is a sure cure for such cases, provided always that they are open to conviction.

In the present plan the control of the Chagres is also effected by a lake, but greater in extent, because the dam is located at Gatun instead of Bohio. This solution was first proposed by Godin de Lépinay, a French engineer, who, in an exhaustive paper on the subject, prepared for the Congress of Engineers in Paris in 1879, advocated the construction of a lock canal with a dam at Gatun in lieu of a sea-level canal. The reasons which he advanced at

THE CUSTOMARY LABORER'S MESS, BEFORE AMERICAN CONTROL

that time were to the effect that such a canal could be built for less money, in less time, and with less sacrifice of life.

THE PRINCIPAL FEATURES OF THE CANAL

The canal which is now building consists of a sea-level entrance channel from the sea through Limon Bay to Gatun, about seven miles long, 500 feet bottom width, and 41 feet deep at mean tide. At Gatun the 85-foot lake level is obtained by a dam across the valley. The lake is confined on the Pacific side by a dam between the hills at Pedro Miguel, 32 miles away. The lake thus formed will have an area of 164

square miles and a channel depth of not less than 45 feet at normal stage.

At Gatun ships will pass from the sea to the lake level, and *vice versa*, by three locks in flight. On the Pacific side there will be one lift of 30 feet at Pedro Miguel to a small lake held at 55 feet above sea level by dams at Miraflores, where two lifts overcome the difference of level to the sea. The channel between the locks on the Pacific side will be 500 feet wide at the bottom and 45 feet deep and below the Miraflores locks the sea-level section, about eight miles in length, will be 500 feet wide at the bottom and 45 feet deep at mean tide. Through the lake the bottom widths are not less than 1,000 feet for about

16 miles, 800 feet for about four miles, 500 feet for about three miles, and through the continental divide, from Bas Obispo to Pedro Miguel, a distance of about nine miles, the bottom width is 300 feet.

The total length of the canal from deep water in the Caribbean, 41-foot depth at mean tide, to deep water in the Pacific, 45-foot depth at mean tide, is practically 50 miles, 15 miles of which are at sea level. The variation in tide on the Atlantic side is 2.5 feet as a maximum, and on the Pacific it is 21.1 feet as a maximum.

Provisions are made to amply protect the entrances of the canal. During the winter months occasional storms occur on the Atlantic side, of such violence that vessels cannot lie with safety in Colon Harbor, and during the progress of such storms entrance and egress from the canal would be unsafe. To overcome this condition, a breakwater will extend out about two miles from Toro Point in a northeasterly direction, which will not only protect the entrance, but will provide a safe harbor. Whether protection on the east side will be ultimately necessary is still an open question.

LABORERS WAITING FOR THE MEAL HOUR
AT ONE OF THE MESSES FOR THE "SILVER ROLL"

To avoid the color question, all employees are divided into two classes, those paid in gold, who form the "gold roll," and those paid in silver, the "silver roll." Americans and Europeans belong to the former, and the West Indians and Panamans to the latter. These men can get a meal ticket for 30 cents after they have done one-half day's work. The meal costs the Commission 27.29 cents.

MESS-HALL AT CULEBRA,
IN WHICH MEN ARE PERMITTED TO EAT WITHOUT THEIR COATS

White laborers can get meal tickets for 40 cents each. The meal actually costs the Commission 36.84 cents. The net weight of the ration furnished the European laborer is exactly equal to the gross weight of the United States Army garrison ration, and the net weight of the ration furnished the black laborer is exactly equal to the gross weight of the United States Army field ration.

The Pacific entrance requires no protection from storms, but the set of the silt-bearing current from the east is at right angles to the channel and the silting made constant dredging necessary. To prevent this shoaling a dike is being constructed from the mainland at Balboa to Naos Island, a distance of about four miles; the benefits derived from it are already very marked.

The projected lakes will submerge the tracks of the Panama Railroad for the greater part of its length, and as this road is necessary for construction purposes, and ultimately for the operation and maintenance of the canal, it is being reconstructed throughout, with the exception of a few miles at either end. It was originally intended to pass the new railroad through Culebra Cut on a berm, 10 feet above the water surface, to be left for this purpose during the excavation of the channel through the cut, but the slides and the absolute necessity for keeping open railroad communication between the

A GROUP OF ITALIAN LABORERS
These men are paid from 16 to 20 cents an hour.

two ends of the line necessitated a change in the location, and a new line to the east of the cut has been selected.

In order to hold its concession the French company continued work on the canal up to the time that the United States assumed control, and after the transfer of rights and property was formally made the excavation was carried on by the United States with the various tools and appliances then in use.

MAKING THE ISTHMUS HEALTHY

The first two and a half years of American control were given to preparation. All energies were devoted during that time to rid the Isthmus of disease by sanitation, to recruiting and organizing a working force, and providing for it suitable houses, hotels, messes, kitchens, and an adequate food supply; to assembling the plant to do the work; to increasing the capacity of the existing railway system, and to establishing a system of civil government for the Canal Zone, which is a strip of land 10 miles wide (five miles on either side of the center of the canal), extending across the Isthmus.

The work of sanitation included clearing lands, draining and filling pools and swamps for the extermination of the mosquito, the establishment of hospitals for the care of the sick and injured, and the quarantine. In addition, to secure and maintain better health conditions, municipal improvements were undertaken in the

SPANISH LABORERS ON THE CANAL

The popularity of the work on the Isthmus has become so great that it is no longer necessary for the Canal Commission to bring in shiploads of recruits from the West Indies and Europe. Laborers are so attracted by the good pay, fair treatment, and excellent living conditions that more than 2,000 came from Spain and Italy during 1910. Old laborers who had left the work to go to Brazil and South American countries have also been returning to the Isthmus in large numbers, seeking re-employment. There are at present about 35,000 on the rolls of the canal works.

SLEEPING QUARTERS FOR EUROPEAN LABORERS,
SHOWING THE THREE ROWS OF "STANDEE" BUNKS

The Commission maintains about 150 houses in which approximately 5,700 European bachelor laborers are quartered.

cities of Panama and Colon, and the various settlements along the line of canal, such as the construction of reservoirs, with mains and adjuncts, for furnishing wholesome and sufficient water, sewerage, pavements, and a system of roads.

Buildings to the number of 2,009 were constructed, including office buildings, hospitals, hotels, messes, kitchens, shops, storehouses, and living quarters. In addition to this, 1,536 buildings out of a total of 2,200 buildings turned over by the French were remodeled and repaired for use.

Recruiting agencies were established in the United States, Europe, and the West Indies.

AN IMMENSE DEPARTMENT STORE

The Commissary Department of the Panama Railroad Company was enlarged until it is now a great department store supplying to the employees whatever may be necessary for their comfort and convenience. Manufacturing, cold storage, and laundry plants were established and turn out each day about 90 tons of ice, 14,000 loaves of bread, 2,400 rolls, 250 gallons of ice-cream, 1,000 pounds of roasted coffee, and 7,500 pieces of laundry. Four to five refrigerator cars, loaded with meats, vegetables, and such fruits as can be obtained, are sent out on the night freight to distant points, and every morning a supply train of about 16 cars, of which number six to eight are refrigerator cars, leaves Cristobal at 4.30 to distribute food-stuffs and laundry to the local commissaries along the line, where the employees make their purchases and where the hotels, messes, and kitchens secure their supplies for the day.

The construction plant, consisting of steam shovels, locomotives, cars, unloaders, spreaders, track-shifters, pile-drivers, cranes, dredges, steamboats, tugs, and barges, was purchased for the most part "knocked down," and shops for their erection and repair were constructed and enlarged. Some of the machinery was built from parts manufactured in the shops. The distance from the home market, with attendant vexatious delays in securing parts and material and the necessity for keeping the construction plant in the most efficient condition for economical operation, made it imperative that the shops be equipped to meet every possible contingency.

The capacity of the Panama Railroad, over a large part of which the spoil from Culebra Cut must be handled, was increased by double tracking it throughout, except from Cristobal to Gatun and from Culebra to Paraiso. Yards were enlarged and connections made to areas available for dumping grounds.

Laws were framed, and civil government was established with its necessary adjuncts of courts, police force, fire companies, customs and revenue service, post-offices, public works, and treasury.

A purchasing department was organized in the United States for the obtainment of supplies of all kinds and descriptions. Upon arrival on the Isthmus, the supplies are shipped to the various subdivisions of the canal-work for which they were purchased, or they are

placed in storehouses along the line for issue when required.

It was only after these various yet necessary adjuncts had been provided and the forces for their operation were organized that the principal work in hand—the building of the canal—could be pushed forward with any hope of success, and too much praise cannot be given to those who conceived and established them in a working condition.

The Department of Construction and Engineering is divided into three construction divisions. The Atlantic Division embraces the engineering construction from deep water in the Caribbean Sea to include the Gatun locks and dam; the Central Division extends from Gatun to Pedro Miguel, and the Pacific Division from Pedro Miguel to deep water in the Pacific Ocean.

KEEPING THE FLOODS OUT OF CULEBRA CUT

As already noted, the Americans continued the work in progress by the French in the cut through the continental divide, commonly known as the Culebra Cut, utilizing the French machinery until it could be replaced by more modern appliances. This is the most formidable part of the enterprise on account of the magnitude of the cutting, and also because of the difficulties attending it, due to the excessive rainfall and to the varying character of the materials encountered.

The efficient and economical working of the plant requires that provisions be made for the disposition of the large quantities of water that result from the rains. Whatever water is not carried off by the streams enters the cut, either through direct fall over the excavated area or by seepage into it. Proper drainage of the cut is therefore an ever-existing problem, and two distinct phases are presented, viz:

1. To keep out the water of the surrounding country.

2. To rid the excavated area of the water that collects in it.

A system of diversion channels accomplishes the first, and gravity drains and pumps solve the second. The canal line follows the Obispo River, which drains the area from the divide to the Chagres River. It has four principal tributaries, two from the east, the Masambi and the Sardinilla, and two from the west, the Mandinga and the Comacho. These are cared for by two diversion channels.

On the east side of the cut the Obispo diversion has been constructed almost parallel to the canal and carried through a depression in the hills so as to discharge into the Chagres about one mile above the point at which the canal line crosses the river.

To the west of the cut the Comacho diversion carries the waters from Culebra to the Chagres River through the old channel of the Obispo River. Through a hill between Haut Obispo and Bas Obispo, which sharply deflects the river, the French had built a tunnel for diverting the flood waters, and this forms a part of the new diversion.

The canal follows the Rio Grande on the southern slope of the divide, and its waters are cared for by a diversion channel constructed by the French. They also constructed a dam across the valley, impounding the waters, and the re-

A TYPICAL LABOR TRAIN

Locomotive engineers are paid from $180 to $210 a month in United States currency; locomotive firemen from $50 to $60 a month, and common laborers from 10 cents to 20 cents an hour.

100,000-GALLON REINFORCED CONCRETE RESERVOIR, BUILT ON NAOS ISLAND
FOR THE CULEBRA ISLAND QUARANTINE STATION AT A COST OF $5,064: 1910

sulting reservoir supplies the settlements from Culebra to and including Panama. During the wet season the diversion channel carries the overflow from the reservoir.

HOW THE SHOVELS WORK

The French so planned the excavation that after the removal of the peak of the divide and lesser summits they could work a number of excavators simultaneously at several points, so that a succession of benches resulted, lying one above the other, each with the natural surface as the point of beginning. By working in the direction of the length of the cut, the face of the bank gives the longest cutting possible, reduces the number of times the excavator must be

hauled back, and secures a satisfactory drainage arrangement, since the cutting is carried up grade on either side of the summit.

The Americans have followed this same method, the only difference being in the character of machinery used. The width of the channel adopted by the French was 74 feet; the present plan is for a channel 300 feet at the bottom, so that the first work undertaken by the Americans was directed to securing the necessary widths for the upper reaches before attempting any increase in depth.

Whatever water entered from rains and seepage was drained from the summit of the cutting by gravity to the Rio Grande on the

DITCH CLEANED BY HAND LABOR,
SHOWING CONDITION TWO MONTHS AFTER CLEANING

south and to the Chagres River on the north. As shovels in excess of those required for widening became available, they were put to work to secure increased depth, care being taken to maintain, as far as possible, free, easy, and rapid drainage. Shovels are started at either end and carried towards each other, cutting out at a new summit. These pioneer shovels on the next lower grade make the "pilot cuts," which constitute the new drains and to which water is led by laterals from various parts of the excavated area adjacent. The average grade or slope is about 36 feet per mile. The loading tracks for these shovels are on the level above.

When the "pilot cut" has progressed sufficiently far, its cut or trench becomes the loading track for a second shovel, which is started to widen out the cut already made by the pioneer, and so the work moves forward, the shovels approaching the summit from either direction in echelon.

In 1904 the summit of the excavation was at Gold Hill and at reference 193 above sea level. The summit at present is between Empire and Culebra and is at reference 106 above sea level. The drainage to the south is still by gravity, through the old bed of the Rio Grande to the west of the Pedro Miguel locks. It is ex-

CONDITION OF DITCH TWO MONTHS AFTER GRASS-BURNING

pected that before the next wet season the center culvert of the locks will be utilized.

On the north side conditions are now different. The reference of the low-water surface of the Chagres is 43 at the point of its intersection with the center line of the canal. The bottom of the completed canal is at reference 40. A dike separates the cut from the Chagres, but this is overtopped during the high floods. To get rid of the accumulated flood water, 24-inch pipes are laid through the dike, each with a suitable valve, and so arranged that all water above the pipes is carried into the Chagres by gravity after the subsidence of any flood.

Recourse must be had to pumping whatever water remains from the floods below this level, and such as may be collected by drainage from the south; for this purpose a sump has been dug to elevation 32 and pumps installed. It is not possible to estimate the quantity of water that will have to be handled, but three pumps are in place, each capable of discharging 12,000 gallons of water per minute.

VERY TROUBLESOME SLIDES

The greatest difficulty encountered in the excavation is due to slides and breaks, which cause large masses of material to slide or move

SWAMP NO. 4, MOUNT HOPE, NEAR COLON,
SHOWING THE ARRANGEMENT OF OPEN-EARTH DRAINS USED FOR SWAMPY AREAS

The sanitary department expended $88,500 in 1910 for maintaining existing ditches and to construct new ones, $127,923.28 in brass and brush cutting, and $72,424 for the removal of night soil and garbage.

into the excavated area, closing off the drainage, upsetting steam shovels, and tearing up the tracks. The term "slide" is applied to the movement of the overlying clay upon smooth, sloping surfaces of rock or other material harder than the clay.

"Breaks" occur at points where the underlying rock is of poor quality, intersected by vertical seams or seams sloping toward the canal, and which is unable to bear up the superimposed mass. Generally, the upper surface of the broken portion of the bank remains approximately horizontal, settling nearly vertically. The weight of the broken portion forces up and displaces laterally the material lying directly below it in the bottom or on the berms of the canal. As the material thus forced up is taken away the upper part gradually settles and moves toward the axis of the canal until the entire broken portion is removed.

The greatest slide is at Cucaracha, and gave trouble when the French first began cutting, in 1884, and still continues. Though at first confined to a length of 800 feet, measured along the line of excavation, the slide has extended to include the entire basin south of Gold Hill or for a length of about 3,000 feet. The original slide covered an area of about six acres, but the latest surveys show that it has extended to cover 47 acres.

METHOD OF EXCAVATION FOR STORM SEWER, "D" STREET, COLON, JULY, 1910

Before the Americans assumed control of the canal there were no sewers and no water system in the Zone. Panama, Colon, and all the towns along the line of the canal have since been provided with excellent water, and sewers for the principal sections have been constructed.

NO DANGER FROM SLIDES
AFTER CANAL IS COMPLETED

There are all told nine "slides" and "breaks" to be reckoned with, and there is nothing to do but to remove all the material embraced within their limits. As the cut is deepened these may be aggravated or others may develop. There is no method known to stop or to prevent them. Usually the first indication received, if there be a forewarning, is the lifting or moving of a shovel and tracks.

The cut has therefore developed into the uncertain and experimental feature of the work and its completion will mark the date of finishing the canal. No apprehension is felt because of the slides after the completion of the work. They develop as the depth of the cut increases, and the banks slide or break because of the condition of unstable equilibrium that results from the cutting; when grade is reached equilibrium will be established, and the back pressure of the water will result in greater stability. Whatever slides occur subsequently will be relatively small, and the material can be easily handled by steam shovels on the berms that will be left and by dredges that will be available.

A NEARLY COMPLETED SECTION OF THE STORM SEWER IN "D" STREET,
COLON, JULY, 1910
The lower half of the sewer is round and the upper half square.

Some idea of the magnitude of the slides can be obtained from the fact that during the fiscal year 1909, of 14,325,876 cubic yards removed, 884,530 cubic yards, or 6 per cent, were from slides. For the fiscal year 1910, of 14,921,750 cubic yards that were removed, 2,649,000, or 18 per cent, were from slides or breaks that had previously existed or that had developed during the year.

THE MATERIAL IS
ALL ROCK

Except for the slides, which are of earth, the material to be removed is rock, and requires blasting to enable the shovels to handle it expeditiously. The largest part of the drilling is done by churn or well drills, though tripod drills replace them where the others cannot be used to advantage. The drills are operated by compressed air, supplied by three compressor plants, which are connected together by a 10-inch pipe line about five miles long, with 6-inch and 4-inch leads running into the cut. The drills operate in batteries of from 4 to 12; the holes, from 15 to 27 feet in depth, are spaced from 6 to 16 feet apart.

The explosive used is dynamite, 45 per cent to 60 per cent nitro-glycerine. Excessive mois-

COLON HOSPITAL GROUNDS, NURSES' HALL, AND QUARTERS FOR PHYSICIANS

As the result of the care of the sanitary department, the health of the workmen is steadily improving. The daily average of sick in 1910 was 23.01 out of every thousand employed, compared to 23.49 for 1909, and 23.85 for 1908. The number of deaths among employees was 548, equivalent to an average of 10.84 per thousand, which would compare very favorably with the death rate of a similar class of people anywhere in the Temperate Zone. No cases of plague or yellow fever originated on the Isthmus. The deaths from typhoid fever among employees were only sixteen, one of whom was white and fifteen black, a remarkable record.

ture and water in the holes prevent the use of blasting powder. When the holes in any section are ready for blasting, they are "sprung"— that is, four to six sticks of dynamite are lowered to the bottom and exploded—thereby forming a chamber for the reception of the charge. The charges vary from 25 to 200 pounds, depending upon the local conditions; the tamping follows, and the explosion is effected by an electric current from one of the lighting plants.

THE EARTH AND ROCK FROM THE CULEBRA CUT ARE USED FOR THE BREAKWATERS AND EMBANKMENTS

Through the blasted area the steam shovel cuts its way, averaging 34 feet wide at the bottom and 50 feet at the top for the "pilot cuts," which are 8 to 12 feet deep. The widening cuts are about 26 feet wide and from 15 to 24 feet deep.

The best results are secured with the 95-ton shovels, though the 45-ton and 70-ton shov-

UNLOADING DYNAMITE FROM SHIP AT PIER 13, MOUNT HOPE, CANAL ZONE: 1910

Last year 14,742,400 pounds of dynamite and blasting powder were shipped to the Isthmus for work on the canal; 350,000 tons of material, valued at $10,103,552.34, were received from the United States during 1910. The value of local purchases, including coal and oil, was $2,094,131.02—345,185 tons of coal and 465,921 barrels of fuel oil were used.

els are also used. The 95-ton shovels have dippers of four and five yard capacities, the former removing rocks containing as much as six cubic yards.

When the rocks are too large to be lifted by the shovel, they are "dobie" blasted, and thus broken to sizes convenient for the dipper. This is done by placing three or more sticks of dynamite on the rock, covering them with mud and igniting by means of a slow match.

The shovels load the material on dirt trains, consisting of 20 flat cars and from 25 to 35 steel side dumps to a train. The available dump grounds in the vicinity of the cut were utilized to their fullest capacity by the French and during the earlier periods of American control, so that longer hauls are necessary.

The new line of the Panama Railroad, being above the lake level, requires many heavy embankments, which offer suitable places for depositing material. The breakwater from Balboa to Naos Island offers a dump, though requiring an average haul of 11 miles.

As difficulty is experienced in extending this breakwater, additional dump tracks are pro-

QUARTERMASTER'S CORRAL AT ANCON, BUILT IN 1910
This is the largest corral on the Isthmus; 600 horses, ponies, and mules are owned by the department.

vided at Balboa, so as not to delay the trains, and land at the inner end of the breakwater is being reclaimed; already 253 acres have been filled in. The interior swamps in the vicinity of Ancon are also to be filled. From 16 to 22 trains of material are sent daily to Gatun, an average haul of 25 miles, and used in building up the toes of the dam or for large rock to place in the concrete. The remainder of the excavated material is wasted on extensive dumps at Miraflores. A large dump ground at Tabernilla was used, but is abandoned for the present.

The Lidgerwood flats are dumped at Miraflores, Balboa, and on the relocated line of the Panama Railroad, where special equipment is kept to handle them, consisting of plows, unloaders, spreaders, and track-shifters. The plow is attached to one end of the train, and the unloader, consisting of a steam-driven drum on which is wound the cable, at the other end. To stretch the cable, the train passes between two uprights to which the cable is attached temporarily, and by moving the train the cable is drawn from the drum to the plow to which the end of the cable is attached. Winding the cable on the drum draws the plow the length of the train, removing the load.

After the material is plowed off, the spreader performs its functions, and, when no longer capable of throwing the material beyond the edge of the dump, the track is shifted by a device patented by W. G. Bierd, formerly general manager of the Panama Railroad, which raises by one motion the track with the ties so

CULEBRA CUT, OPPOSITE TOWN OF CULEBRA, LOOKING NORTH, JUNE 10, 1910,
AFTER A HEAVY RAIN OF ONE HOUR

There is a record of 5.86 inches of rainfall in one hour.

as to clear the ground, and by another motion pulls it sidewise. The usual throw is two and a half to three feet, though, if the rails will permit, the track can be thrown as much as nine feet in one throw (see page 69).

The steel dump-cars require no special or extra appliance for their operation, and can be dumped as easily on curved as on straight track. They also dump to either side.

Work has been in progress on the Culebra Cut since 1880, and during the French control 18,646,000 cubic yards were removed. Between Gatun and Bas Obispo, the northern end of Culebra Cut, the French excavation which is useful to the present project amounted to 2,201,000 cubic yards, or a total in the Central Division of over 20,000,000 cubic yards. The total estimated amount of material to be excavated from May 4, 1904, in this division was 97,125,018 cubic yards, of which, up to January 1, 1911, 67,792,855 cubic yards have been removed, or 69.7 per cent. It is expected that all the excavation in the lake section will be finished by July 1, 1911.

Some idea of the magnitude of the operations may be formed from the fact that this division has within its jurisdiction over 200 miles of 5-foot-gauge track laid, about 55 miles of which are within the side slopes of the Culebra Cut alone.

SPRAYING CRUDE OIL IN DITCHES TO EXTERMINATE THE MOSQUITOES
The sanitary department spent $43,000 last year for the purchase of oil and to pay laborers to distribute it.

THE GREAT DAM AT GATUN
IS A VERITABLE HILL

An earth dam across the Chagres at Gatun impounds the water of the river and creates the lake which constitutes the summit level. The dam is 7,500 feet long over all, measured along the top, and, according to the latest profile, it is 2,100 feet wide at the base, 398 feet through at the water surface, reference 85, and 100 feet wide at the top, which is 115 feet above sea-level. It crosses two valleys separated by a hill rising to elevation 110, in which the regulating works are being constructed. Of the total length of the dam, only 500 feet will be exposed to the maximum head of 85 feet, the remainder to less.

The dimensions of the dam have been criticised as excessive and unwarranted, but its designers considered it desirable, in view of the amount of material available, that ample provisions be made against every force which may affect its safety, and that a barrier be made so that the layman without engineering knowledge would recognize its stability. Now that the dam is assuming appreciable proportions, this latter object is more than realized.

The dam in plan is a broken line to conform to the configurations of the natural surface, thereby materially reducing the fill. It extends from the hill in which the locks are to be constructed to Spillway Hill, thence along the

STEAM SHOVELS SUBMERGED IN THE CUT
AT BAS OBISPO DURING A FLOOD
(SEE PAGE 70)

THE CHAGRES RIVER BREAKING THROUGH A PROTECTION DIKE
AND FLOODING THE CANAL (SEE PAGE 57)
The Chagres River has been known to rise 25.6 feet in 24 hours.

spur or hog-back of the hill on the west side of the valley (see map, page 87).

The adoption of the earth dam brought on such criticism that an exhaustive examination of the foundations was made in order to determine more carefully the character and extent of the various underlying materials; to ascertain whether there was any possible connection between the swamp areas to the north and south through the deposits in the gorges across which the dam will be built; for testing the ability of the material to support the proposed structures, and for learning whether suitable material for the dam could be obtained in the immediate vicinity.

As the result of the investigations, it may be briefly stated that the underlying material is impervious to water; that it possesses ample strength to uphold the structure that will be placed upon it, and, the subsoil being impervious, that there is no connection between the swamps above and the sea below.

Because of the sluggish current of the river in the vicinity of Gatun and above, the deposits consist of the finer sands and silts interspersed with beds of clay. By constructing experimental dams of this material and subjecting them to the full head of water, it was conclusively demonstrated that this material is suitable for the interior or the impervious core.

DEPOSITS OF SAND AND GRAVEL BROUGHT DOWN
BY HIGH FLOODS OF THE CHAGRES RIVER IN NOVEMBER AND DECEMBER, 1909

The dam is constructed by forming two dumps on the outer lines of the structure and depositing waste material, mostly rock, obtained from Culebra, the lock site, and Mindi. The area between the piles thus formed is filled with the material pumped in by hydraulic dredges, the natural surface of the ground having been previously cleared of vegetation and a suitable bonding trench excavated.

THE SPILLWAY

Fluctuations in the lake due to floods are to be controlled by regulating works constructed in Spillway Hill. Objections were made to constructing such works in the line of the dam, but because of the natural configuration of the ground, irrespective of the location of the spill-

way, provision had to be made for tying the dam to the sides of the hill; moreover, the extent and elevation of the hill, as well as the material composing it, make it a suitable and desirable place for the waste weirs. The channel has been cut, the floor and side walls of concrete completed, and the Chagres River now discharges through it. As the reference of the floor is at 10 feet above sea-level, the lake is already formed at least to this height.

The spillway dam will be of concrete with its crest at elevation 69. Piers 8.5 feet wide will be built on top of the crest, 53.5 feet centers, grooved for Stoney gates, which will close the openings and complete this portion of the dam. The trace of the dam will be the arc of a circle 740 feet long, with 14 openings, which, when

TRACK-RAISING AND SHIFTING MACHINE

This powerful machine lifts the track and ties clear of the ground and then deposits them from three to nine feet away. It bends the steel rails as easily as if they were made of clay (see page 63).

the gates are raised to the full height, will permit a discharge of 140,000 cubic feet per second. The water discharged over the dam will pass through a diversion channel into the old bed of the Chagres. (See map, page 87.)

The dam is to contain 21,145,931 cubic yards of material. On January 1, 1911, there had been placed 12,001,592 cubic yards, making 56.72 per cent of the dam complete. The spillway will contain an estimated quantity of 225,485 cubic yards of concrete, of which 113,269 cubic yards, or 50.23 per cent, were completed on January 1.

THE LOCKS
CAN BE FILLED OR EMPTIED
IN 8 MINUTES

The locks are in pairs, so that if any lock is out of service navigation will not be interrupted. Thus, also, when all the locks are in use, the pas-

CUT AT EMPIRE, LOOKING NORTH

In the upper right-hand corner is seen the break in the rock bank which let the Obispo diversion into the canal for three days, drowning out some of the shovels at the north end. This break aggregates about 40,000 cubic yards, but will not be disturbed until the dry season. A flume has been constructed of timber and concrete to carry the flow of the diversion past the break.

sage of shipping will be expedited by using one set of locks for the ascent and the other for descent. The locks are 110 feet wide and have usable lengths of 1,000 feet.

The system of filling adopted consists of a culvert in each side wall feeding laterals perpendicular to the axis of the lock, from which are openings upward into the lock chamber. This system distributes the water as evenly as possible over the entire horizontal area of the lock, and reduces the disturbance in the chamber when the latter is being filled or emptied. (See diagram, page 88, and illustrations, pages 92-93.)

The middle or separating wall contains a single culvert of the same area as the culverts in the side walls, which feeds in both directions through laterals controlled by valves designed to operate against a head from either direction. This arrangement permits communication between the chambers of twin locks, so that water may be passed from one lock to the other of the pair, effecting a saving of water. The main culverts are controlled by Stoney valves, and the laterals leading from the center wall by cylindrical valves.

Assuming a difference of head of 30 feet, it is estimated that the entire lock can be filled or

BREAK IN THE WEST BANK OF THE CANAL AT CULEBRA

Note the successive benches on which the shovels work. Nearly one-fifth of all the material removed from
Culebra Cut in 1910 was from slides and breaks like this.

emptied, using one culvert in 15 minutes and 42 seconds, and in 7 minutes and 51 seconds when both culverts are used.

The lock gates are of the mitering type, double leaf, straight gates, varying in height from 45 feet 7 inches to 79 feet; the length of each leaf is about 65 feet. A contract has been entered into for furnishing the steel for the gates and for their erection in place by June 1, 1913. To meet this condition, it is necessary that the concrete work shall be completed in time to enable the contractors to begin the erection of the various sets of gates on the dates specified in their contract, and the work is being prosecuted with this end in view. To accomplish the re-

sult, the concrete for the Gatun locks must be finished by June 1, 1912, and that for the locks on the Pacific side by October of the same year.

SAFETY DEVICES

It has been accepted as a fundamental feature of the design that at each flight of locks there must always be two barriers separating the high level from the level next below. To carry this out, two sets of mitering gates are placed at the upper and two at the lower end of each of the uppermost locks in each flight.

In addition a chain device is used to guard the barrier gates against accident, and so controlled as to be capable of checking a ship of

ANOTHER VIEW OF THE BREAK IN THE WEST BANK AT CULEBRA,
SHOWING FOUR STEAM SHOVELS WORKING ON THE BROKEN AND MOVING MASS

The two upper shovels are casting material over the berm, to be loaded by the two lower shovels into the Lidgerwood train. This break has necessitated the removal of nearly 2,000,000 cubic yards.

10,000 tons moving at the rate of about five miles an hour.

More than 95 per cent of the vessels navigating the high seas are less than 600 feet in length, and this has been taken as the determining factor for the location of intermediate gates, which are introduced in the design to save both time and water. For the protection of the intermediate gates against vessels using a smaller length of chamber a chain barrier is to be installed.

Guide piers are provided both upstream and down, to which vessels will tie before entering the locks. Designs for electric towing machines are being prepared, which will be used for towing vessels into and controlling their passage through the locks by means of lines or cables attached to what may be considered the four corners of the ship.

Even with all of these precautions accidents may happen, and emergency dams are provided at the head of each flight of locks, consisting of swing bridges, which can be thrown across the locks in case of an accident which makes a connection between the top level and the level below; wicket girders are let down

BREAK IN THE EAST BANK OF THE CANAL, OPPOSITE CULEBRA, JUNE, 1910

from these swing bridges, supported by a sill at the bottom and the horizontal truss work of the bridge at the top. These wicket girders act as runways for gates, which are lowered and gradually stop the flow.

GATUN LAKE WILL STORE WATER FOR THE DRY SEASON

It will not be out of place at this point to give consideration in a general way to the question of adequacy of the water supply to maintain a large commerce through the locks. Data bearing on the subject have been collected for many years and studied with care. During eight or nine months of the year there is more than a sufficient supply for all purposes, but during the other four or three months there is practically none, and it becomes necessary to store a sufficient quantity during the rainy season to supply the needs during the dry season.

The enormous reservoir of Gatun Lake is available for this purpose. The bottom of the canal in the summit level is at reference 40, and it is evident that navigation, with the extreme depths provided of 40 feet in sea water, can be carried on until the surface of the lake falls to reference $81\frac{2}{3}$. As the water surface in the lake is to be allowed to rise to reference 87, there is stored available for the dry season a little more than five feet.

BREAK IN THE EAST BANK AT CULEBRA

Showing how the pressure of the broken bank, shown in the preceding picture, has raised the bottom, for a short distance, to a height of 18 feet above its original level (see pages 57 and 61). A similar break advanced 14 feet in 24 hours, overturning the steam shovels and disheartening the men. There is no way to prevent these breaks.

Making due allowances for power consumption, evaporation, about which data are available, seepage and leakage at the gates during a dry season of minimum flow, assumed as following a wet season of minimum flow, an average of 41 passages of the canal per day is possible, using the full length of lock. In the average dry season 58 complete transits of the canal are possible, or a greater number than the 24 hours of the day would permit, allowing vessels to follow each other at intervals of one hour.

With the design for the locks as adopted a certain amount of water can be saved at each lockage whenever a vessel does not draw the full permissible depth of 40 feet by cross-filling or emptying through the middle wall. As a consequence it can be stated that there will be sufficient water for as many lockages as the time in the day will permit.

INGENIOUS METHODS
FOR HANDLING THE ROCK AND CEMENT

At Gatun three locks in flight overcome the difference in level between the lake and sea, and are being constructed in a cutting made through a hill. The excavation, consisting of upwards of

CULEBRA CUT, LOOKING NORTH

5,000,000 cubic yards, mostly rock, is practically completed. The locks are of concrete, and contain about 2,046,100 cubic yards of this material. On January 1 last they were 49 per cent completed.

The broken stone for the concrete is quarried and transported from Porto Bello, about 20 miles east of Colon, and the sand is procured from Nombre de Dios, about 20 miles farther to the east. Both are transported direct to Ga-

tun in barges through the French Canal, which was dredged of rock ledges and accumulated deposits for the purpose. Since the canal line was cut through to the French Canal this new channel is also used. The cement is purchased under contract at docks in Jersey City and shipped to Cristobal, thence by barges to Gatun or cars to Pedro Miguel and Miraflores.

The material taken to Gatun in barges is landed at unloading docks, conveniently lo-

A TEMPORARY TRESTLE ACROSS THE BRAZO BOTTOM, LOOKING SOUTH

One of the most difficult tasks connected with the canal is to relocate and rebuild the Panama Railroad, and at the same time not to interfere with the tremendous traffic across the Isthmus. The large lake which is being created by the Gatun Dam will completely submerge the present railway for the greater part of its length. This illustration shows a depression, across which an embankment nearly a mile long, and containing 1,500,000 cubic yards of earth and rock, must be built to hold the railway above the level of the lake.

cated on the old east diversion, to which a channel from the French Canal was excavated by dredges. The east dock is inclosed, forming the cement storehouse. Its floor dimensions are 106 feet by 490 feet. The roof projects 35 feet beyond the face of the dock, affording some protection against the rains.

The building is divided into ten bays, in each of which a two-ton traveling crane, worked by electric motors, operate entirely across the building. In the rear of the building 30 cement hoppers are placed in the floors and covered with steel screens. The cement is delivered through these hoppers into cars running on a track below the floor. The cement for this work is in barrels, which are first put into the storehouse and subsequently moved to the hoppers.

Grab buckets, operated by cableways, remove the sand and stone from the barges, moored against the west dock, and deliver the materials in stock piles. The towers of the cableways are of steel, 85 feet high and 800 feet apart. They are mounted on cars, which enable movement at right angles to the line of the cable; one

RELOCATING THE PANAMA RAILROAD ACROSS THE VALLEY OF THE GATUN RIVER:
THIS EMBANKMENT WILL BE THREE-FOURTHS OF A MILE LONG
AND CONTAIN 1,000,000 CUBIC YARDS

single and two duplex cableways are provided. (See illustration, page 82.) Each of the latter have complete independent cableway systems. The cableways are equipped with five 70 cubic feet self-digging grab buckets, each having an independent run from the barge to the stock pile. The cableways have not the capacity to unload the material required with sufficient rapidity, and have been augmented by three derricks operating on a dock north of the cement shed, transferring sand and stone to bins.

THE AERIAL CABLEWAYS

Two tunnels run north and south through the stock piles, with hoppers in the top through which stone and sand are fed to cars.

The cars used for transferring the material are of steel with hinged side doors, and bottoms inclined outward at an angle of 52 degrees from the horizontal. A steel partition divides each car into compartments, one for rock and cement and one for sand. The car starts at the cement shed, where it receives two barrels of cement, thence runs through one of the tunnels, receiving a full charge of stone and sand in the proper compartment, and proceeds to deliver this load in the mixer hopper.

The concrete mixers are of the cubical type, each having a capacity of 64 cubic feet. There are eight of them, all mounted in one building on the west side of the lock site, arranged so that

BUILDING GATUN DAM BY HYDRAULIC FILL:
LIFT, 63 FEET; LENGTH OF PIPE, 4,300 FEET

The dam is constructed by forming two dumps on the outer lines of the structure and depositing waste material, mostly rock, obtained from Culebra, the lock site, and Mindi. The area between the piles thus formed is filled with the material pumped in by hydraulic dredges, the natural surface of the ground having been previously cleared of vegetation and a suitable bonding trench excavated.

four dump in one direction and the other four directly opposite, thus permitting the use of two tracks under the mixers. There is, however, but one track above.

A four-track electric railway, third-rail system, operates the length of the locks and carries the concrete from the mixers to the cableways over the locks, by which it is placed. The equipment for this road consists of 12 electric four-wheel mine-locomotive-type engines and 24 flat cars fitted with automatic couplers, each designed to carry a two-yard concrete bucket.

Two charges of concrete are taken by each train and carried to the cableways.

Four duplex cableways span the locks with steel towers 85 feet high and 800 feet apart, similar in design to the unloading cableways.

The forms used in concrete laying are of steel and, for the straight portion of the walls, so designed as to permit construction of monoliths 36 feet in length extending from the floor to the top of the walls. The forms for the main and the lateral culverts are of steel and are collapsible.

FROM GATUN TO THE OCEAN

The channel from the locks to deep water in Limon Bay, approximately seven miles in length, is being excavated in part by steam shovels and the remainder by dredges.

South of the French Canal the Mindi Hills cross the line of our canal between Gatun and Limon Bay, rising to the elevations 50 and 60. As the bulk of the excavation is rock, steam shovels were put to work to secure the requisite width and depth. It was thought that when sea-level was reached the shovels would have to be replaced by dredges, as the Mindi River is within a few hundred yards of the area, and the French Canal borders it. As the work progressed, however, notwithstanding the seamy nature of the rock, it was found that a relatively narrow levee would keep out water from the French Canal, and the seepage was so small as to be easily handled by pumps. One shovel-cut to grade was made, when the high water in December, 1909, flooded the pit and work was suspended until recently, when the soft material was removed by a suction dredge. The water is being pumped from the pit so as to permit completion of the work by steam shovels.

VIEW OF PORTO BELLO QUARRY, ABOUT 20 MILES EAST OF COLON, SHOWING CRUSHING PLANT AND SHIPPING BINS

This plant, owned by the government, supplies the crushed stone for the concrete work at Gatun. The amount of stone quarried and crushed in the fiscal year 1910 was 549,678 cubic yards, at an average cost for the last six months of $2.6283 per cubic yard delivered in the stock-pile at Gatun, this cost including plant charges and division expenses. The greatest month's output was in June—a total of 74,184.

To handle the millions of tons of stone, sand, and cement required for building the locks, ingenious machinery has been installed which automatically selects the right proportions of stone, sand, and cement and mixes the material. The piles in the foreground in the above picture are sand; the darker piles on the further side of the railway track are stone. Grab-buckets shoot down from the arms of the crane, bite into the piles, shoot back to the crane, and feed their loads into the mixer, where cement has been already delivered in bags or barrels.

Over the area to be dredged, a seagoing suction dredge removes the softer material, while ladder and dipper dredges handle the rock and stiff clays. The underlying rock is drilled and blasted prior to dredging. A total of over 35,000,000 cubic yards was the estimated amount to be excavated, of which 60.3 per cent is completed.

THE LOCKS AT PEDRO MIGUEL

In the Pacific Division the work consists of the construction of duplicate locks at Pedro Miguel overcoming a 30-foot difference of level,

with the necessary dams; two locks in flight, also in duplicate, at Miraflores, connected with the adjacent hills by one earth and one concrete dam; excavating the channels between the locks to the required depths, and the excavation of the channel to proper width and depth to deep water in the Pacific.

The Pedro Miguel locks connect the summit or 85-foot level with the 55-foot level. The excavation for the locks, amounting to 770,000 cubic yards, is completed, and of the 837,400 cubic yards of concrete required for their construction, 57 per cent is completed.

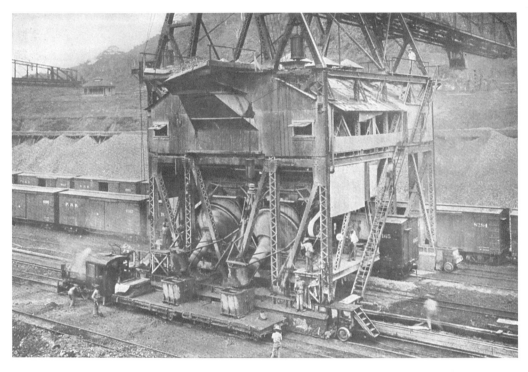

ONE OF THE AUTOMATIC CONCRETE MIXERS LOADING CONCRETE IN BUCKETS

The government has contracted for 4,500,000 barrels of cement for the various locks, dams, and structures of the canal. If these barrels were placed in a single line touching each other they would reach from New York to Denver.

The west dam connects the head of the locks with the hills to the northwest and performs the same function at the south end of the lake that the Gatun dam does at the north. It is to be of earth, about 1,400 feet long, 40 feet wide at the top, which will be at reference 107 above mean tide, and have side slopes of 8:1. It will be subjected to a maximum head of 40 feet, though the average head is from 25 to 30 feet.

In its construction two rock piles are formed; between these two masses of material (from which an existing stratum of gravel was removed), selected material will be placed properly puddled and rolled. This central portion will have a thickness of 140 feet at the bottom. Concrete core walls will connect the dam with the hill and lock. The dam, which contains about 1,000,000 cubic yards, is 26 per cent completed. The natural surface of the ground from the east wall to an adjacent hill is above the upper level, but it is to some extent pervious to water. To cut off any possible flow, the lock wall is returned toward the hill, with which it will be connected by a concrete core wall.

THE LOCKS AT MIRAFLORES

The Miraflores locks are two in flight, overcoming the difference in level between Miraflores Lake, whose surface is at reference 55, and the sea-level section. As the fluctuations in tide are about 20 feet and mean tide is the datum, it will be noted that the maximum lift for these locks is about 65 feet. The excavation for the upper set of locks is complete and for the lower set it is about 70 per cent complete. It was not intended to lay any concrete until the plant at Pedro Miguel had finished the locks at that locality, but, as the work has advanced so much more rapidly than anticipated, and as the contractors are to complete the erection of the gates seven months earlier than expected, it became necessary to install auxiliary mixers and begin this part of the work earlier. There will be a total of 1,312,200 cubic yards of concrete to lay for these locks, of which 7 per cent is already done.

The Cocoli River, a tributary of the Rio Grande, crosses the site of the Miraflores locks from the west, and is such a formidable stream in times of heavy freshets that the protection of the locks against its floods during construction and after completion is necessary. A diversion channel through the hills to the west with a dam

GENERAL VIEW OF UPPER LOCKS AND FOREBAY, GATUN, LOOKING NORTH, IN 1909

Four duplex cableways span the locks, with steel towers 85 feet high and 800 feet apart. They pick up from the delivery car the big buckets of concrete, send them out on the aerial trams, and lower them where required. One man operates a cableway, controlling all the movements by switches located on a platform on each head tower. In addition to delivering concrete in the locks, the cableways are used to lift material from the lock site and dump it by an aerial dumping device, to handle forms for the concrete work, and to handle the parts of the gates and the gate-operating machinery. The carrying cable is a locked steel wire 2¼ inches in diameter, its carrying capacity being considerably over 6 tons. Twenty trips an hour can be made on each cableway. The greatest lift is 170 feet. The towers are set on tracks on which they can be easily moved along the lock site as the work progresses.

ANOTHER VIEW OF THE AERIAL CABLEWAYS USED AT THE GATUN LOCKS:
LOOKING NORTH FROM EAST BANK, AUGUST 25, 1909

This illustration shows the early stages of the construction of these locks. The two "squares" on the left are timber forms in which concrete was laid in sections for the foundations. The uprights on the right are old French rails imbedded in the concrete to reinforce the floor. The floor of the Gatun locks varies in thickness from 13 to 20 feet of solid concrete reinforced with these rails.

across the river valley would accomplish the desired end; but, as a dam at the head of and to the west of the locks is also necessary to impound the water for the pool above, the solution finally adopted was the construction of a dam extending from the head of the locks to Cocoli Hill, with a direction nearly parallel to the axis of the locks; by this arrangement the Cocoli River will discharge into the upper pool.

The dam is of earth, 2,300 feet long, top width 40 feet at reference 70, and the side slopes approximately 12:1. The average head to which the dam will be subjected is 30 feet, the maximum 40 feet. It is being constructed like the Gatun dam, and is 43 per cent complete. The east dam will be of concrete, approximately 500 feet long, provided with regulating works similar to and of the same dimensions as those at Gatun, the crest in this instance being at elevation 39, with seven openings, permitting a discharge of 7,500 cubic feet per second.

BUCKETS OF CONCRETE READY TO DESCEND
AND BE PLACED BY THE MEN WAITING BELOW

This view of the upper locks at Gatun (looking south from the middle lock) was taken December 30, 1910, and shows the walls of the twin upper locks practically completed. Note the steel forms (1) for the construction of the walls.

For a distance of one and one-half miles south from the Miraflores locks rock is found in the channel, to be excavated at an average elevation of minus 30. The estimated quantity to be removed is 1,503,260 cubic yards, which is covered by 8,158,133 cubic yards of alluvial material, averaging 38 feet in depth. It was not practicable to remove the earth and rock by dredging and subaqueous methods, as the requisite plant could not have been assembled to complete the work in the allotted time.

An hydraulic excavating plant was, therefore, selected as being the cheapest and most expeditious method of handling the loam, especially because by this means 450 acres of swamp land adjacent to the canal could be reclaimed. Four hydraulic pumps force water through pipes, fitted with hydraulic giants or monitors, with a pressure of 130 pounds per square inch at the nozzles; these jets wash the loam to sumps, from which 18-inch centrifugal dredging pumps, mounted on reinforced concrete barges, pump the material to such places as may be desired.

Below the area to be excavated in this manner, the channel is secured by ordinary dredg-

RECEIVING THE CONCRETE

Note the men standing on top of the wall on the extreme left. The largest amount of concrete laid in any one month at Gatun is 89,401 cubic yards. The average cost of the concrete per yard in place for 1910 was $7,355, including plant charges and division expenses. To build the Gatun locks 2,250,000 barrels of cement will be required.

THE EAST CHAMBER OF THE UPPER LOCKS AT GATUN, LOOKING SOUTH:
DECEMBER 16, 1910

Note the steel towers for holding the face forms, which in this view are shown moved away from the wall preparatory to removal to a new location. Each lock at Gatun is 110 feet wide and has a usable length of 1,000 feet.

ing operations. Rock encountered is blasted, the drilling being done by churn drills through the natural surface to the proper depth or, where submerged, by use of a drill scow. A Lobnitz rock breaker is also in use for preparing the rock for the dredges. The total amount of material to be excavated aggregates 35,000,000 cubic yards, of which 73.55 per cent is completed.

REBUILDING THE RAILROAD

The relocated Panama Railroad is being pushed forward so as to keep pace with canal construction work. From Colon to Mindi and from Corozal to Panama, the old line, relieved of some of its curvature, will be used, but the remainder must be rebuilt. From Mindi to Gatun, two miles, and from Paraiso to Corozal, four miles, the new line is completed and is being operated.

Just south of Miraflores the new road passes through a tunnel 800 feet long. The section from Frijoles to Gamboa, 9 miles, is complete to grade and has been turned over to the Central Division for use in wasting material. This includes a steel bridge across the Chagres nearly one-quarter of a mile long. From Gatun to Fri-

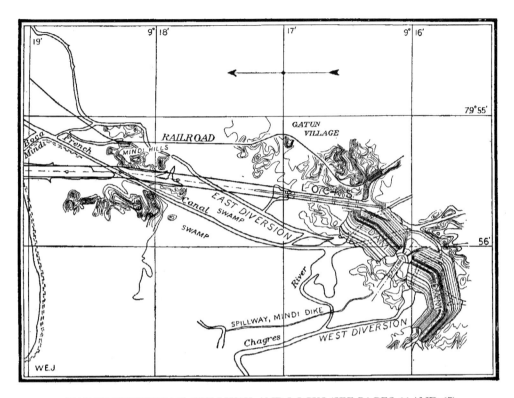

MAP OF GATUN DAM, SPILLWAY, AND LOCKS (SEE PAGES 66 AND 67)

joles a temporary line was completed up to grade 60 in April, 1910, and maintained ready for operation at any time during the past wet season that the old line was flooded out.

About 3,000,000 cubic yards are still required to complete the embankments of this section to elevation 95, and every effort is being made to finish the entire line to Gamboa, 31 miles, to full grade by January 1, 1912. On this date it is expected that work in the Gatun spillway will have progressed sufficiently to begin raising the lake to elevation 55.

Construction of the line from Gamboa to Paraiso, east of the cut, was started in January and will be pushed with a view to completion by January 1, 1912, if possible. As the greater part of the road passes through the lake, reinforced concrete culverts are provided to equalize the water on both sides of the embankments.

THE CANAL WILL BE COMPLETED ON TIME

Generally speaking, employees are selected on account of their special fitness for the work in hand, and are then unhampered in their methods of securing definite results, thus bringing out to its fullest extent individual effort and brain power. As a consequence each man has a

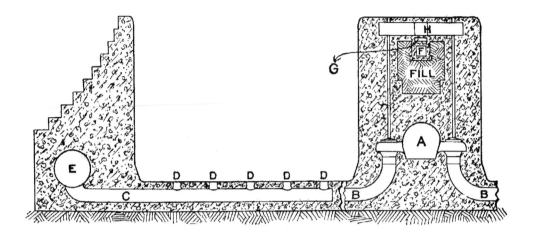

CROSS-SECTION OF LOCK CHAMBER AND WALLS, GATUN LOCKS

A. Culvert in center wall.
B. Connections between center and lateral culvert.
C. Lateral culvert.
D. Wells opening from lateral culverts into lockchamber.
E. Culvert in side wall.
F. Drainage gallery.
G. Gallery for electric wires.
H. Passageway for operators.

There will be three main culverts extending the full length of the locks, one in each of the side walls and one in the middle wall. The side-wall culverts are 22 feet in diameter from the intake at the south end of the upper locks to a point 320 feet north, where they are reduced to 18 feet, at which diameter they will continue to the end, a distance of about 3,500 feet. The culvert in the middle wall is 22 feet in diameter from its south end to a point 120 feet north, where it also will be reduced to 18 feet, at which diameter it will continue to the end, a distance of about 3,600 feet. Lateral culverts in the form of an ellipse will run in the floor from and at right angles to the main culverts at intervals of 32 and 36 feet, leading alternately from the side and middle culverts. Water will be delivered or collected by each lateral culvert through five openings or wells in the floor. Valves, which may be opened or closed either individually or all at one time, will be located at the intakes and outlets of the main culverts, and at the connections between the center culverts and the lateral culverts (see page 90). In the center space of the middle wall there will be a tunnel, divided into three stories or galleries. The lowest gallery is for drainage; the middle, for the wires that will carry the electric current to operate the gate and valve machinery, which will be installed in the center wall, and the top, a passageway for the operators.

personal interest in the work and seems imbued with the idea that the success of the enterprise depends on him. The spirit of enthusiasm and of loyalty among the canal workers strikes forcibly every one who visits the Isthmus, and convinces the doubting that the canal will be built.

The time required for completing the lock type of canal was estimated by the Board of 1905, which made its report in January, 1906, at 9 years, in accordance with which the work should be completed by January 1, 1915, and this is still retained as the date for the official opening. The expectation that the locks will be completed by June 1, 1913, is dependent on the gate contract and has already been noted, which leaves Culebra Cut as the doubtful factor.

THE MIDDLE WALL OF THE GATUN LOCKS

The size of the structure can be appreciated by noting the man at the bottom. The great cylinder is the culvert to fill or empty the locks (see page 70).

DIAGRAM TO SHOW PROPORTION OF EXCAVATION OF CANAL ALREADY COMPLETED

The quantity remaining to be excavated may, however, be considerably increased by slides into Culebra Cut. The figures are cubic yards.

THE SIDE WALL OF ONE OF THE GATUN LOCKS COMPARED TO A SIX-STORY BUILDING

The size of the culverts may be appreciated from the engine and dray. The "steps" will be filled in with earth and stone and graded to the top. Face forms for the side and center walls (see preceding illustration) are of sheet steel carried on movable towers, also built of steel. Tracks are laid as near to the line of the walls as possible, and on these tracks the towers move up and down the lock chambers parallel with the walls (see page 86). Jacks fixed to the towers and bearing on the forms are used to align the forms and hold them in place. There are 12 of these towers, with forms 78 feet long from top to bottom, 36 feet wide, and 7½ inches thick (see page 84).

THE SLIDES
IN CULEBRA CUT ARE
THE ONE DOUBTFUL FACTOR

Assuming that all the material will slide into the cut that was estimated in June last, so that all of it will have to be removed, it is estimated that this part of the cut will be finished by September 1, 1913. It is well within possibility—indeed, it is probable—that other slides or breaks will develop, and it may be more economical to admit the water, thus getting the advantage of the back pressure, and remove the remainder by dredges, which will then be available and which can be passed through the locks when completed. This will be done if need be, but in any event there is nothing that can be foreseen at present which will postpone the date fixed for the official opening, with ample time to spare for tuning up the operating machinery and to organize and train a force for the operation and maintenance of the canal by January 1, 1915.

The great barrels are the steel collapsible forms for the culverts in the side wall. The steel towers in the distance hold the face forms (see page 86). Forms for the culverts are made of open-hearth boiler steel, are collapsible, are mounted on wheels to facilitate withdrawal, and are constructed to stand five years of continual use. For the main culverts in the side walls there are 21 forms in 12-foot lengths, each form weighing not less than 14,443 pounds. There are 12 forms for the culvert in the middle wall, each 12 feet long and weighing not less than 14,750 pounds. There are 100 forms for the lateral culverts, each 10 feet long and weighing not less than 2,170 pounds.

PLACING THE FORMS FOR THE LATERAL CULVERT IN THE MIRAFLORES LOCK

ANOTHER VIEW OF THE FLOOR OF THE MIRAFLORES LOCK, SHOWING THE OPENINGS
TO THE CULVERTS BY WHICH THE LOCK WILL BE FILLED AND EMPTIED

VIEW OF THE PEDRO MIGUEL LOCKS, LOOKING SOUTH FROM THE EAST BANK:
AUGUST 30, 1910

The steep banks on either side make the arrangement of aerial cableways used at Gatun impracticable, and hence these chamber cranes are used. Each crane is mounted on four heavy freight-car trucks, which carry it along as the work progresses. All the machinery is in the house on top of the tower.

With concrete work in the locks coming to a close in the early part of 1912, steps must be taken to disband the present organization. The time has arrived for outlining an organization for the operation and maintenance of the canal. The tuning up of the machinery and the training of an organization will require the actual use of the canal. It is stated on reliable authority that at least 18 months will be required for shipping to adjust itself to the new conditions that will exist when the canal is ready for use. Such readjustment, however, will not be attempted until some definite announcement is made of the tolls that are to be charged and the basis for such tolls.

THE CANAL IS WORTH
THE $375,000,000 INVESTED

Much has been said and predicted as to the commercial value of the canal to the United States. In this connection it must be remembered that the commercial shipping of this country never required the canal. The trip of the Oregon in 1898 settled the question of the advisability of constructing an Isthmian Canal, and had the canal been built at that time, thereby saving that trip around the Horn, there is no question that it would have been agreed generally that the canal, even at an expenditure of $375,000,000, was worth while.

A VIEW OF THE PEDRO MIGUEL LOCKS (LOOKING NORTH FROM THE SOUTH END)
TAKEN DURING A FLOOD: DECEMBER, 1910

The isthmus is not 50 miles wide where the canal cuts it, and yet the rainfall varies to an extraordinary degree in this short distance. At La Boca, on the Pacific, the average fall recorded for 12 years is 69 inches per year, while at Bohio the average for 13 years is 130 inches per year, and at Christobal, on the Atlantic, 128 inches per year for a period of 38 years. The months of January, February, and March are practically rainless. In the seven months from May to November, inclusive, 85 per cent of the rainfall occurs.

In whatever light the Panama Canal is viewed, it will have paid for itself if in time of war or threatened war a concentration of the fleet is effected without that long, tedious, uncertain route followed by the Oregon.

It will practically double the efficiency of the fleet, and, notwithstanding the fact that we are a peaceful nation, our outlying possessions make the Panama Canal a military necessity, and it must be so recognized. From this point of view the debt should be charged to the account

which necessitated its construction, and whatever revenues are derived from other sources are so much to the good. The traffic that will utilize the canal depends upon the tolls that will be charged, and the President has asked the Congress for legislation which will enable the establishment of rates.

There is another policy which if adopted will have a material bearing on the revenues of the enterprise. Through the Panama Railroad a large expenditure of money has been made for providing the present working forces with supplies of all kinds. Though the railroad has been reimbursed for this plant through fixed charges on sales, it should not be abandoned, but utilized for furnishing shipping with its needed supplies. Suitable coaling plants should be erected for the sale of coal to vessels touching at or passing through the canal. In addition, since oil is now used on a number of ships plying in the Pacific, such fuel should also be on hand for sale by the canal authorities.

The extensive machine shops now located at Gorgona must be moved before the completion of the canal, and they should be established in connection with a dry dock that will be needed for commercial purposes, and utilized as a revenue producer for the canal. This policy also needs congressional action.

With properly regulated tolls, and with facilities for fully equipping, supplying, and repairing ships, the Panama route would offer many advantages and bring to it a sufficiently remunerative return to pay not only the operating expenses, but to gradually absorb the debt which the United States has incurred by its construction.

THE PANAMA CANAL*

By Lieut. Colonel William L. Sibert, U. S. Army

Engineer in Charge of the Atlantic Division

THE Panama Canal, as all know, is being built by the President of the United States through a commission of seven members, the chairman and chief engineer of which is Col. George W. Goethals, of the Corps of Engineers, United States Army. As a member of the commission and as division engineer of the Atlantic Division, I have had charge of the construction of the Gatun locks, the Gatun Dam, the breakwaters in Colon Harbor, and the excavation of the channel between the Gatun locks and the Atlantic Ocean.

If there are any people who yet hold the idea that the waters of the Atlantic and Pacific will mingle in this canal, I think that two statements of fact will dispel that idea forever.

*An address to the National Geographic Society, November 29, 1913

One of the statements is that for about 32 miles this canal is 85 feet above the level of the Atlantic and Pacific. The second statement is that water will not flow uphill.

HOW THE CANAL IS DESIGNED

What has really been done is that a great dam has been built across the lower end of the valley of the Chagres, entirely blocking the flow of that river to the sea. The height of the dam and spillway is so fixed that the Chagres River will rise and rise until it reaches a stage 85 feet above the level of either ocean. At this stage the Chagres River will form a lake 165 square miles in area and 45 feet above the bottom of the cut that has been made through the Continental Divide at Culebra.

The Chagres, therefore, can flow into both oceans—to the Atlantic through the locks at Ga-

A VIEW ON THE CHAGRES RIVER

It is the Chagres River that has made the Panama Canal possible. It supplies the water for the Gatun Lake—the largest artificial lake in the world—across which the vessels will steam for nearly two-thirds of the entire distance from coast to coast.

tun and to the Pacific through the locks at Pedro Miguel and Miraflores. The water of the Gatun Lake not needed in passing ships through the locks goes to the Atlantic Ocean through a spillway (see page 113).

THE BREAKWATERS AT COLON

Starting at the Atlantic side, the first work that has been done is the construction of the west breakwater at Colon. It was thought that that breakwater would be sufficient to insure a safe harbor. The line of the canal at Colon is due north and south, and the most destructive storms, the "northers," are from a little west of north; so that the west breakwater will provide a safe anchorage for ships during such storms.

The prevailing winds at Colon, however, are the trade winds, that blow from the east or

ON THE UPPER CHAGRES

This picture gives some idea of the many beauty spots found along the banks of the Chagres River.

north and continue for more than nine months of the year. These winds do not produce a sea destructive to shipping, but they make a rough harbor, stir up the soft bottom of Limon Bay and create currents, with the result that there is a large amount of silting in the channel through the bay. For two years in succession this silting amounted to more than two million cubic yards of material.

In order to remedy this condition, and for other reasons, it has been decided to construct an east breakwater also. Its end will be opposite the end of the west breakwater, leaving an opening of 2,000 feet. When this breakwater is completed, the silting in the channel will cease and all difficulties of transfers from one boat to another in the harbor will be eliminated. The west breakwater should be completed in the summer of 1914, and the work on the east breakwater has just commenced.

HOW THE BREAKWATERS ARE BUILT

The method of building the breakwaters is as follows:

A trestle, suitable for a double-track railroad, was driven from the shore, extending for two miles out to sea. The rock forming the bottom of the breakwater was run out on cars and dumped or plowed off until the fill was made alongside the trestle to an elevation of 15 feet below sea-level. Between that level and 10 feet above sea-level the breakwater was built of hard trap rock, obtained from Porto Bello, the stone ranging in weight from 1,500 pounds to 15 tons.

The stone for the armor of the breakwater, as well as all crushed stone for the Gatun locks, came from this seacoast town of Porto Bello, situated some 20 miles northeast of Colon.

This place has given all kinds of trouble. The first year we attempted to crush stone for the Gatun locks, we had at Porto Bello a rainfall amounting to 237 inches—3 inches less than 20 feet; 9 feet of rainfall in two months; 58 inches in one month.

Everything happened at Porto Bello that could happen. Slides that no engineer would dream of occurring did occur. On an average 300,000 cubic yards of crushed stone every day were necessary for the concrete at Gatun. We had a young officer of engineers there, Captain

SPORT ON THE CHAGRES

One of the diversions very popular among the sporting members of the canal staff was alligator hunting. The upper waters of the Chagres could usually be relied upon to produce excellent sport, though these great reptiles are found in all the principal streams on the Isthmus.

Stickle, who was doing the best he could, but we were pushing him anyway; so, after he had been urged and urged and then urged again to do more, one day he sent a wireless, "Fifty-eight inches of rain this month. Anything over fifty inches considered an act of God."

THE FRENCH CANAL
WOULD HAVE BEEN USELESS NOW

A little to the north of the Gatun locks the American and French canals intersect, and the picture on page 102 shows the relative sizes of the two. Had the French canal been completed it would now be out of date, for its locks would not be of a size sufficient to pass the boats that would now offer.

In the French project the sea-level part of the canal on the Atlantic side extended about 10 miles farther up the Chagres Valley than the American project. The water supply would have been materially less than in the American plan and would not have been sufficient for the substitution of locks of the size now built, and those now adopted are none too large to meet the requirements of Congress that the Panama Canal should be built of such size as reasonably to meet the demands of the future as to the size of ships.*

The canal is at sea-level from the Atlantic to Gatun; it then goes up a flight of three steps to Gatun Lake and continues at that level for 32 miles. Then down one step at Pedro Miguel

*The full length of each lock compartment is 1,000 feet. The largest ship in the world, the *Vaterland*, of the Hamburg-American Line, which is not yet completed, has a length of 950 feet. While it is unlikely that the huge liners used in the transatlantic passenger service will often be required to pass through the canal, still the locks are big enough to accommodate the largest ship in the world.

to Miraflores Lake, which is 55 feet above sea-level; thence through the Miraflores locks, and the canal from there to the Pacific is at sea-level again.

The proudest day that Gatun has yet had was on the 26th day of September, 1913, when the little tugboat *Gatun* was lifted from sea-level to the surface of Gatun Lake, and was the first boat to pass through any lock of the Panama Canal (see page 105).

As soon as a boat passes the lower lock gates they are closed behind it, and water is let into that box or lock chamber from the lock above until the same level of water exists in the lower and middle locks, the boat being lifted 28⅓ feet in this operation. After that the gate separating the lower and middle lock will be opened and the boat will pass into the second lock, the gates closed behind it, and the process repeated, the boat being lifted another 28⅓ feet. That operation repeated once more will cause the boat to float out on the level of Gatun Lake.

The filling of the lower chamber of Gatun lock for the first time is shown in the picture on page 107. The gate on which all the men are standing is called the east gate or guard gate. These gates were completed as soon as practicable and then closed, so as to keep the sea out of the locks while dredges were completing the excavations in the lock entrance, thus not interfering with the work on the other gates nor with the machinery installation.

PAINTING MOSQUITOES

On both sides of the channel at Gatun were extensive swamps. They were great breeding places for mosquitoes, and in digging the channel through the soft, swampy bottom pipe-line dredges were used. These dredges cut up the

A COMPARISON OF THE FRENCH AND AMERICAN CANALS

This is a picture looking toward the Atlantic Ocean from the Gatun locks at the point where the present canal crosses the French excavations. Had the French canal been completed, it would now be out of date, as it was much smaller than the present one and its locks would not be of a size sufficient to pass the large ships of the present day.

material near the suction of the pumps, draw it in with water, and force it long distances through pipe-lines. In making the channel excavation those swamp areas were built up high enough to enable the sanitary department to drain them.

In 1912 Gatun had probably the greatest influx of malarial mosquitoes in its history; they came by the thousands. The Gatun Lake was rising at that time, and it was not known whether these mosquitoes were coming from that lake or not; so the sanitary department determined to locate all the breeding places for mosquitoes near Gatun, catch mosquitoes at each place, and after painting them turn them loose, and determine by the color of the mosquitoes caught in Gatun from what point they came.

It was found that the largest breeding place was off to the west of the locks, in an old swamp that had given no trouble previously. A few mosquitoes had bred in this place all the time, but there were enough wild animals in the swamp to supply food, so the mosquitoes were not forced to migrate. When salt water was pumped into the swamp water, making the mixture about 30 per cent salt, mosquitoes began to breed by the trillions.

I went down there one morning to see how the mosquitoes were caught and painted. Walking along the edge of the water, mosquito bars were seen suspended from limbs tied up at the bottom. They had thousands of mosquitoes in them ready to be sprayed with a colored liquid, and the military inspector was asked how he caught them.

He said, "We have a more scientific way, but this had to be done in a hurry. We simply let the mosquito bar down, as you would over a bed, left one side of it open, and put a Jamaica negro in there for bait." As soon as the mosquito bar was full the bait was removed and the end tied up.

I saw some Jamaican negroes sitting out in front, and I said to one fellow. "John, were you the bait in that bar ?" and he replied, "Yes, boss; that is the easiest money I ever earned—ten cents an hour for sitting there and doing nothing but just inviting the mosquitoes in."

THE DREDGING FLEET

Just prior to the time that water was let into Culebra Cut, a fleet of dredges was brought up preparatory to removing Cucaracha slide, the last one that obstructed the passage across the continent. The picture on page 110 shows part of the fleet assembled for passing through the locks, and gives a good picture of a pipe-line dredge, showing the cutter in front. When this cutter is revolved, those blades loosen the dirt, the intake of the pump is just behind, and when the water is drawn in by the pump it carries in from 15 to 20 per cent of solid matter, and the pump gives it velocity enough to be carried from one-half to three-quarters of a mile through a pipe.

The entire dredging fleet is shown in the picture on page 111. There were about ten vessels of various sorts in one lock chamber, and even then it was not full. Attention is especially called to one piece of plant in the fleet, and that is the old French dredge, a ladder dredge distinguished by the endless chain with buckets. This old French dredge has served loyally two administrations and is still in the advance guard going to attack Cucaracha slide. By a peculiar coincidence, M. Bunau Varilla, the former chief engineer of the French Canal Company, passed through the locks during this event aboard one of the boats in the fleet. He, as you know, was a great advocate of a sea-level canal.

More precautions have been taken probably in the Panama Canal locks than in any other locks in the world. In addition to having duplicate gates at each end of the lock, a great chain is attached to a system of hydraulic cylinders and kept in the position shown until a boat makes a landing alongside the guide wall and a towing locomotive takes charge of it. Then the chain is lowered into a groove in the bottom of the canal. This fender chain across the entrance is shown in the picture on page 112.

THE FLOATING ISLANDS OF GATUN LAKE

A large part of the bed of what is now Gatun Lake was formerly swamp land. In that swamp were logs on which grass and small trees had grown. When the lake rose, the entire bottom floated. The wind broke it into pieces, sometimes an acre or more in extent, and since

THE GATUN LOCKS, LOOKING TOWARD THE ATLANTIC

The waters of the Atlantic flow into the canal for seven miles, until they reach the first gates of the lower lock at Gatun. The lower and middle locks are shown in the picture, while the incline leading to the upper locks appears in the foreground. The swamps in the distance at the left were a constant source of trouble while the locks were being made, owing to the innumerable mosquitoes which bred in them (see pages 101-103).

that time these pieces have been floating aimlessly about the lake (see page 115).

During the fall of 1912 the water was allowed to flow 6 or 7 feet deep over the uncompleted spillway, and a large number of these floating islands were passed over it. As soon as the lake reaches normal height and water can be spared, these floating islands will be towed systematically to the spillway and passed over and out to the Atlantic.

As the waters of the Chagres River came down and encountered the dam at Gatun the lake was gradually formed, and during this process much vegetation was submerged. As the lake rose it gave the ladies of Panama great opportunities for collecting orchids.

The most beautiful orchids have a way of growing on the largest trees, and so high that they are difficult to get; but while the lake was rising to 85 feet above sea-level, one could row around in small boats through the trees and pick them off (see pages 116 and 117). A Kipling should have been at Panama to write a jungle story that would describe the action of the wild animals when this great permanent flood of the Chagres came.

THE LOCKS AT GATUN, LOOKING IN THE OPPOSITE DIRECTION
TOWARD GATUN LAKE

These are the upper locks at Gatun, where vessels lie during the last of the three stages of being lifted from sea-level, on the Atlantic side, to the level of the Gatun Lake, 85 feet above, after which there is 32 miles of clear sailing before Pedro Miguel, the first lock on the Pacific side, is reached. Beyond the locks we see Gatun Lake, 16.5 square miles in extent. Note the floating islands.

The last natural barrier that held back the water of Gatun Lake from the cut that had been made across the Continental Divide was the dike at Gamboa. Up to this point the canal has followed the Chagres Valley. It now leaves the valley and cuts across the Continental Divide to Pedro Miguel, and there commences to go down the Pacific slope.

The Gamboa dike was broken down on October 10, 1913, by the explosion of a charge of dynamite which had been stored in it. This charge was fired by the depression of a tele-graph key in the White House at Washington by President Wilson (see page 118). Before the dike was blown up, water was allowed to enter the Culebra Cut through pipes, so as to fill it to within 5 or 6 feet of the level of the lake. Had it been blown up with 30 feet difference in level, some damage might have resulted.

THE CULEBRA CUT AND THE SLIDES

The Culebra Cut will, it is thought, be the most striking of all the features of the canal. The Gatun Lake, when all the trees are gone, will be beautiful with its green islands and green promontories: but the most striking feature, I think, will always be the great cut across the Continental Divide.

The most difficult slides to handle have occurred in that part of the canal near the Continental Divide, marked by Gold Hill and Contractor's Hill, all comprised in a length of about 1½ miles of canal. Just beyond Gold Hill is the famous Cucaracha slide, the surface of which was above the lake level when the water entered Culebra Cut, and it prevented the water from flowing through the cut to Pedro Miguel.

An unsuccessful attempt was made on the same day that the dike at Gamboa was destroyed to blast a channel through this slide. A ditch, however, was finally made across it, through which that part of the canal between Cucaracha and Pedro Miguel was filled with water. This allowed dredges to be towed from the Pacific end of the canal to assist those already brought from the Atlantic side in completing the channel excavations.

FIRST BOAT THROUGH THE GATUN LOCKS

One of the memorable days in the history of the Panama Canal was September 26, 1913, when the tugboat *Gatun* was lifted from sea-level to the surface of Gatun Lake, being the first boat to pass through any lock on the canal.

The Cucaracha slide has broken back to the crest of the hill behind Gold Hill, a half a mile or more from the prism. Since the slide is now broken back to the crest of the hill, and since the face of the hill away from the canal is being artificially removed, a fairly close calculation can now be made as to the number of cubic yards of material that can slide into the canal from that source and the approximate time that it will take to remove it.

A large part of the material composing this slide is clay, and it is hoped that it can be removed by pipe-line dredges. By placing a relay pump in the pipe-line, material can be forced over the banks of the canal. The pipe-line dredge is very efficient in digging and transporting material away from the site, providing the distance or lift is not too great. Material can be so transported from a half to three-quarters of a mile with great ease.

One of the dredges getting ready to attack the Cucaracha slide from the south is shown in the picture. This dredge came from the Pacific side, and across the slide can be seen the smoke-stack of the dredge that came from the Atlantic through the Gatun locks. It is hoped that within two or three months a channel can be made of sufficient width and depth for the passage of ships. However, no one who has served on the canal would try to make a definite prediction.

OPERATING THE GATUN LOCKS FOR THE FIRST TIME

The gate on which all the men are standing, while watching the lower chamber of the lock being filled for the first time, is the sea gate or guard gate (see page 101).

THE LOCK GATES

The lock gates are a most interesting feature of the canal. There are 46 of them, each having two leaves, and their total weight amounts to 58,000 tons. They vary in size from 47 to 82 feet in height and it takes no less than six million rivets to put them together. Some idea of their enormous size can be gained by comparing the men working on them with the gates themselves.

Gold Hill is a hard trap rock, with a volcanic neck extending down to an unknown depth, and is there to stay. On either side of it, however, the strata were very much disturbed and slides have occurred of all kinds of material, both clay and rock. The slides on the north side are nearly all of soft rock.

Colonel Gaillard, who had charge of the work in Culebra Cut, never knew, when he returned to work in the morning, that tracks and shovels would be found as left the night before. He struggled with the cut for six long years, until it was practically completed, but finally broke and died under the strain.

Two distinctive kinds of slides are encountered in Culebra Cut. In one case the entire body of material moves practically on an inclined plane, this plane being sometimes rock, sometimes clay. The Cucaracha slide is of this character and is called a true slide.

In slides of the other character, the first indication is a crack in the bank, sometimes 300 or 400 feet back from the edge of the cut. This crack or break opens, and the ground there will often settle down before it does at the edge of the cut. When the general movement comes, the bottom of the cut comes up. Steam shovels have been lifted by one of these slides as much as 18 feet, with the tracks hardly thrown out of alignment.

EARTHQUAKES AND THE CANAL

One of the great arguments against a lock canal at Panama was the earthquake argument, which prophesied that the locks would inevitably be destroyed, by earthquake shocks. The picture shown on page 120 is the answer to that argument. It shows the famous flat arch in the now ruined church of Santo Domingo in Panama City, which has stood there for more than 200 years. The existence of this old and apparently unstable structure is a proof that Panama is free from serious earthquakes.

An examination of this arch, taken in connection with the fact that it has stood for the length of time it has, seems to warrant the conclusion that Panama has been more free from serious earthquakes during the time in question than Tennessee, Missouri, or Arkansas, when it is remembered that Reel Foot Lake, in Tennessee, and the "Sunk Lands," in Missouri and Arkansas, along the basin of St. Francis, were formed during an earthquake in 1812, a little more than a century ago, while this structure has stood for more than twice that period.

Panama has been visited by a few earthquake tremors lately, one of them being of sufficient intensity to cause vases to fall from shelves, but careful examination of the locks failed to show the slightest cracks in the masonry, and the dam showed no tendency to settle or change its form in any way whatever. The center of the disturbances which produce the tremors is usually about 200 or 300 miles away. I do not know where the center of these last disturbances was, but when the serious earthquakes occurred in Costa Rica two or three years ago, only slight tremors were felt at Panama.

While I was away, in November, my wife wrote me that there had been another little earthquake since I left. She was upstairs and had a Jamaican woman sewing at the time, and just as the house commenced to shake the Jamaican woman fell down on her knees to pray. While my wife believes in the efficacy of prayer, she told the woman that the best place to pray during an earthquake was outside. The advice is thought to be good.

THE GATUN LOCKS

All the essential features of the Gatun locks are situated on rock. It is a soft rock and was called indurated clay in the first description of it; but people did not understand what indurated clay meant, and so the name was changed to argillaceous sandstone.

This stone is solid and makes a good foundation when not exposed to the air. If so exposed, however, it acts like shale and goes to pieces. In making an excavation for the locks and as soon as grade was reached, the foundation was immediately covered with concrete, thus reproducing the same condition under which nature has kept the rock sound.

There can be no question as to excellence of the foundation of the locks at Gatun. They are completed and have been subjected to the most trying conditions without the slightest settlement or crack. As stated before, all the es-

ONE OF THE GREAT SUCTION DREDGES ENTERING GATUN LOCKS

This is one of the great suction or pipe-line dredges, showing the cutter in front. When this cutter is revolved the blades loosen the dirt; the intake of the pump is just behind it, and when water is drawn in by the pump it carries in from 15 to 20 per cent of solid matter, and the pump gives it velocity enough to be carried from one-half to three-quarters of a mile through a pipe.

sential parts are on rocks: the only exception is the south guide wall, the one that leads into Gatun Lake. This is built on piles and is of as light construction as possible. It has no particular function except that ships will land on both sides of it.

Prior to the construction of the Gatun locks, many holes were made with a diamond-drill outfit into the rock foundation to depths of 100 feet or more below sea-level in order to ascertain the character of the foundation and determine whether or not the rock was sufficiently

creviced to transmit pressure from the lake to the lock floor. After the holes were bored the ground water showed in them. By pumping the water out of some of the holes and observing to what extent and how quickly the water was lowered in the others, conclusions were drawn as to the probability of the rock being sufficiently creviced to transmit pressure.

These experiments indicated that minute crevices were in the rock, not enough for the passage of any appreciable amount of water, but probably enough to transmit pressure. Consequently the floors in the Gatun locks from the emergency dams to the intermediate gates of the upper locks are so built that if the full lake pressure does come under them they will stand it. Below that, provision is made for carrying any leakage to sea-level through drains behind the lock walls.

In case a ship should break the upper lock gates and the Gatun Lake should start to flow through the flight of locks to the sea, a swing bridge is provided for each upper lock, by means of which an emergency dam can be built across the locks. The operation of these swing-

bridge dams is as follows: The bridge is first swung across the lock chamber and heavy girders are then lowered, one end of each of them finally resting against a sill previously built in the bottom of the lock entrance. Steel curtains are then run down in tiers on tracks on the girders, gradually building a dam and stopping the flow of water. The girders and curtains are all lowered under power and the entire operation can be carried on through swiftly flowing water.

It is purposed to allow no ship to go through the locks of the Panama Canal under

DREDGING FLEET IN THE MIDDLE LOCK AT GATUN

The fleet is on its way to the Culebra Cut to help in removing the Cucaracha slide. The last dredge in the lock is an old French dredge of the ladder type, having an endless chain with buckets. This dredge has served loyally through two administrations and at the end was still in the advance guard. The immense size of the locks can be realized from the fact that there are ten vessels in this lock and yet it is not full.

ENTRANCE TO THE UPPER LOCKS AT GATUN, SHOWING THE GREAT GUARD CHAIN

"More precautions have been taken probably in the Panama Canal locks than in any other locks in the world. In addition to having duplicate gates at each end of the upper lock, a great chain is attached to a system of hydraulic cylinders and kept in the position shown until a boat makes a landing alongside the guide wall and a towing locomotive takes charge of it. Then the chain is lowered into a groove in the bottom of the canal."

its own steam. A ship will be required to land alongside the guide wall at either end of the locks.

Towing locomotives, four of them, will run down the guide walls, pass lines to the ship, two forward and two aft, and will then tow the ship into the locks, hold it during the time it is being raised or lowered, and finally deliver it alongside the guide wall at the other end. This is a precaution that has never been taken before in operating locks. One of the experimental towing locomotives is shown in the picture on page 114.

Ships are ordinarily allowed to pass through locks under their own steam. The wrong ringing of a bell or the misunderstanding of a bell has ordinarily been the cause of wrecking a lock gate.

HIGH AND DRY BELOW SEA-LEVEL

One of the most difficult problems at Gatun was the preparation of a foundation at the lower end of the locks. It was necessary to go 70 feet below sea-level through soft mud to find rock suitable for foundations. The material was so soft that steam shovels could not be supported on it, so it was decided to do the excavation by dredges. A sufficient width of land between the space to be excavated and the canal toward the Atlantic was left to act as a dam when the excavation was finally completed and unwatered.

A dredge was allowed to cut a narrow channel through this dam into the space where the walls were to be built. This dredge dug the entire space to a depth 40 feet below sea-level, which was its limit. A dam was then placed across the narrow entrance cut, with the result that the dredge lowered itself as it continued its work. When it had lowered itself to 30 feet below sea-level, it could excavate to the required depth—70 feet below sea-level.

After completing the excavation, the dredge pumped all the water out of the space, leaving itself grounded 55 feet below the level of the sea, in which position it remained until the walls

THE SAFETY VALVE FOR THE CHAGRES RIVER AND GATUN LAKE:
THE GATUN SPILLWAY

The surplus waters of the Gatun Lake escape to the Atlantic Ocean through this spillway. It is a large semicircular concrete dam, along the top of which are 13 piers, which furnish it with 14 outlets. These outlets are closed by huge steel gates, 45 feet wide and 20 feet high, each weighing 42 tons. Should the Chagres River fill Gatun Lake so full of water as to endanger the locks at Gatun, this spillway would act as the safety valve. Even if the lake rose to the improbable height of 92 feet above sea-level—its normal height is 85 feet—it would not be necessary to open all the gates on the spillway. Three or four of them would carry off all the water necessary to avert danger.

THE LOCOMOTIVES OF THE LOCK

These little electric locomotives, here shown climbing the incline between the middle and upper locks at Gatun, are very powerful and will be used to draw the big ships through the locks. No ship will be allowed to go through the locks under its own steam (see page 114). Note the men at work on the huge lock gates.

were completed. Water was then let in from the sea; the dredge floated and cut its way out (see page 120).

THE GREAT GATUN DAM

Gatun dam, across the Chagres Valley, is about a mile and a half long, a third of a mile thick at the base, with a top elevation of 105 feet above sea-level. A small hill existed in the center of the valley at the dam site. While it was 200 feet below sea-level to rock in the portion of the valley to the east of the central hill and 260 feet to rock in that portion to the west, rock was found at 40 feet above sea-level in the central hill itself—a fortunate condition, because a stable channel for the temporary diversion of the Chagres could be easily cut through this hill, across which channel a masonry spillway, founded on rock, could be built later.

A spillway through an earthen dam is generally looked upon with disfavor. While the Gatun Dam is earthen, it is really two dams, one extending from the locks to this central hill and one from this central hill to the west side of the valley. Rock existing at a high elevation in this central hill made it an ideal location for a spillway or waste weir.

When the building of the Gatun Dam was commenced, the Chagres River was flowing through three channels at the dam site—its own, the old French canal, and a diversion channel dug by the French to the west of Spillway Hill. The first operation was to block the flow of the Chagres through its own channel and through the old French canal, thus forcing all the water through the west diversion channel.

This enabled the work of building the east half of the dam to be started while a channel was being dug through the Spillway Hill. As soon as this latter channel was finished the Chagres River was turned into it by damming the west diversion channel.

The bed of the west diversion channel being below sea-level, with soft banks and bottom, and the bottom of the Spillway channel be-

FLOATING ISLANDS OBSTRUCTING THE LOCK

A large part of Gatun Lake bed was swamp land. In that swamp were logs on which grass and small trees had grown. When the lake rose the entire bottom floated. The wind broke it into pieces, sometimes an acre or more in extent, and since that time these pieces have been floating aimlessly about the lake.

ing 10 feet above sea-level, this last diversion of the Chagres proved to be a troublesome undertaking. As soon as this last diversion was accomplished work on the west half of the dam was commenced.

The watertightness of the Gatun Dam was never a subject of serious apprehension. The material under it and that in the center of it are practically impermeable. The great problem concerning the Gatun Dam has been to make the material on which it was built carry the load.

I referred to the rock being 200 feet below sea-level on one side of Spillway Hill and 260 feet on the other. These old gorges, so the geologists say, were made by the Chagres River when all the country in the vicinity of Gatun was about 300 feet higher than it is now. When the site of the Gatun Dam was lowered 300 feet during some early volcanic disturbance and its old beds lowered 200 feet below sea-level, the sea backed up the Chagres Valley and in time filled these old gorges with deposits, largely of clay, which in some places were soft.

THE DYING JUNGLE IN GATUN LAKE

"As this lake rose it gave the ladies great opportunities for collecting orchids. The most beautiful orchids have a way of growing on the largest trees and so high that they are difficult to get, but as the lake rose to 85 feet above sea-level, one could row around in small boats through the trees and pick them off" (see text, page 104). When this photograph was taken the water had only risen to 52½ feet above sea-level.

THE DROWNING TREES IN GATUN LAKE

When this picture was taken there was only 52½ feet of water in Gatun Lake, but when the lake is full these trees will be entirely submerged.

In order to make such a foundation carry a heavy load. an exceedingly broad base was necessary.

Dams are ordinarily built with quite steep slopes, one in two, or one in three, whereas the Gatun Dam was built with a slope of about one in ten. The foundation was simply spread, making the dam about a third of a mile through at the base, so that the underlying material would carry the load. This underlying material was compressed under the load in some places as much as 15 feet. As the load was gradually placed on it, the material in the base became more and more compact, until finally settlement has practically ceased.

Every two or three months borings have been made through the material in the dam itself, and that under it, for the purpose of ascertaining any changes in the character of such materials. This data shows that the material, both in the dam and under it, is continually becoming more compact. It stands today, safely carrying its full load, and tomorrow it will be able to carry more.

THE JAMAICAN IS HARD TO KILL

The dam was built by constructing trestles in both edges of it and from these trestles making rock fills or "toes." When these toes had reached a height of 60 feet on the south face and about 30 feet con the north, dredges commenced to pump an impermeable mixture of sand and clay in between them. This central core constitutes the real barrier to the passage of water through the Gatun Dam.

As the hydraulic fill was built up the rock fills were carried up, so as always to constitute levees, holding the additional hydraulic fill. A pipe-line dredge pumps about 20 per cent solid material and 80 per cent water, so in building a dam this way it is necessary to provide some means for draining off the surplus water.

This was done where the dam joins the hill, a 20-inch pipe being laid in a trench on the rock and carried in to the lower edge of the hydraulic fill. An elbow was then placed on the end of the pipe, and as the water and hydraulic fill rose other sections were added to the elbow. A cage was placed around the intake end of this pipe to keep the drift away, and men were sent occasionally to remove such drift from the pipe intake.

At one time when water was running through this pipe under a 30-foot head, three Jamaicans were removing drift and one of them

BLOWING UP THE GAMBOA DIKE (SEE PAGE 105)

The last land barrier between the two oceans was broken down on October 10, 1913, by the explosion of a charge of dynamite stored in the Gamboa Dike. The charge was fired by the depression of a telegraph key at the White House by President Wilson.

THE FIRST BOAT THROUGH MIRAFLORES LOCK

The lock-chambers here and at Pedro Miguel are the same size as those at Gatun. At this lock, the last on the Pacific side, boats can be let down to the level of the Pacific from that of the Miraflores Lake, through which the canal runs after leaving the Pedro Miguel locks at the termination of the Culebra Cut. The boat shown in the picture is entering the lock from the Pacific Ocean,

fell in the 20-inch pipe. The other two tried to pull him out but could not. They let him go and ran as quickly as they could to the other end of the pipe. The man traveling in the pipe reached the end first, notwithstanding the fact that he turned a corner at an angle of 90 degrees. His ears were scratched a little!

There was a great deal of emulation between the employees in the different divisions. The part of the story so far told is true, but Colonel Gorgas made the addition that the man jumped up and said that there wasn't anybody on the Pacific Division who could do that.

The spillway over which the surplus waters of the Gatun Lake find their way to the Atlantic Ocean is found on page 113. This is a picture of the spillway when practically complete.

The gates on top are 45 feet wide and the lake will stand 16 feet deep against them when no water is being wasted; consequently if one or more of the gates is lifted water will flow between the piers 16 feet deep. These gates are raised and lowered, like a window-sash. These movable gates constitute the regulating works, by means of which the level of Gatun Lake is controlled.

"THE QUEEN OF AMERICA" AND THE LUNCHEON PARTY

In the beginning but very little provision was made for quarters for families of the canal employees. It soon became evident that order could not be maintained, contentment prevail, and a permanent force kept unless the wives of the men were there; so the commission undertook to build family quarters.

It was announced in circulars, etc., that employees would be provided with family quarters within ten months after arrival on the Isthmus. Not only all the married men immediately applied for quarters, but nearly every unmarried man on the job applied. Family quarters carried with it free light and fuel.

Nearly every one of the young unmarried men the first time they came back from leave brought a wife if they could get one. The building department was consequently overwhelmed and the commission was forced to withdraw its literature and make no promises. An attempt was made after that to provide a certain percentage of the employees with family quarters.

The greater part of the laborers on the canal were Jamaican negroes. They were British

DREDGE GROUNDED 55 FEET BELOW SEA-LEVEL (SEE PAGE 113)

This dredge was used to excavate the foundations of the Gatun lock and dug down 70 feet below sea-level. "After completing the excavation, the dredge pumped all the water out of the space, leaving itself grounded 55 feet below the level of the sea, in which position it remained, until the walls were completed. Water was then let in from the sea; the dredge floated and cut its way out."

FILLING A LOCK

The water enters through a series of apertures arranged in rows of five along the floor of the lock. The barrel-shaped objects on the right of the picture are jets of water which have not burst into spray like those on the left.

subjects, but were ordinarily called "British objects." They make good servants if thoroughly trained and the routine is not varied.

To illustrate the effect of varying the routine: Visitors often came rather unexpectedly for lunch at Gatun, and in order that things might go right if my wife happened to be away when company came, she had prepared menus for lunches—number 1, number 2, number 3, etc. All I had to do was to telephone the cook that so many people were coming and to prepare lunch number so and so.

One day Mrs. Roosevelt and her daughter came with Mr. Bishop to see the work at Ga-

tun, and after asking them to lunch, my wife being away, I telephoned the cook that there would be three extra people and to prepare luncheon number 1. I, unfortunately, said that Mrs. Roosevelt would be there.

The Jamaican has great respect for royalty. Before reaching home I heard that our servants had passed the word around among the other servants at Gatun that the Queen of America would take lunch at our house today. On entering the house it was evident that every piece of cut glass, silver, or pretty China in the place was out where it could be most easily seen.

On reaching the table it was soon seen that we had lunches 1, 2, and 3 combined. But finally, when four tiny cups of coffee were passed on a large salver resurrected from an old chest upstairs, the ridiculous side of the situation was complete.

Now that the canal is essentially finished, what are the American people going to do with it? Shall the new markets brought into existence on the Pacific shores of Central and South America by this new cheap transportation route be supplied by the United States or by foreign countries?

In my judgment, that depends, more than anything else, upon whether the Congress of the United States enacts such laws as will bring into existence a United States merchant marine engaged in foreign commerce.

THE FLAT ARCH AT PANAMA

One argument against the construction of a lock canal was that the great locks at Panama might be destroyed by earthquakes. This flat arch, which any serious earthquake shock would destroy, has stood for nearly three centuries in the now ruined church of Santo Domingo at Panama, proving that fear of earthquakes is groundless (see page 109).

FURTHER READING

David McCullough, *The Path Between the Seas: The Creation of the Panama Canal, 1870-1914* (1977) is a fact-filled account of this unprecedented engineering feat. Walter LaFeber, *The Panama Canal* (1989) focuses on the diplomatic issues involved in building the Canal. See also, Edmund Lindop, *Panama and the United States: Divided by the Canal* (1997).

An excellent book for younger readers is Elizabeth Mann's *The Panama Canal* (1998).

INDEX

CONTRIBUTORS

General Editor FRED L. ISRAEL is an award-winning historian. He received the Scribe's Award from the American Bar Association for his work on the Chelsea House series *The Justices of the United States Supreme Court*. A specialist in American history, he was general editor for Chelsea's *1897 Sears Roebuck Catalog*. Dr. Israel has also worked in association with Arthur M. Schlesinger, jr. on many projects, including *The History of the U.S. Presidential Elections* and *The History of U.S. Political Parties*. He is senior consulting editor on the Chelsea House series *Looking into the Past: People, Places, and Customs*, which examines past traditions, customs, and cultures of various nations.

Senior Consulting Editor ARTHUR M. SCHLESINGER, JR. is the preeminent American historian of our time. He won the Pulitzer Prize for his book *The Age of Jackson* (1945), and again for *A Thousand Days* (1965). This chronicle of the Kennedy Administration also won a National Book Award. He has written many other books, including a multi-volume series, *The Age of Roosevelt*. Professor Schlesinger is the Albert Schweitzer Professor of the Humanities at the City University of New York, and has been involved in several other Chelsea House projects, including the *American Statesmen* series of biographies on the most prominent figures of early American history.